To Timothy, with Love, from Grandma Bale
2013

HOW TO

HANDLE

YOUR LIFE

D0048733

HOW TO HANDLE YOUR LIFE

Carine Mackenzie

CF4·K

How to Handle your Life ISBN 978-1-85792-520-3

© Copyright 2008 Carine Mackenzie

Published by Christian Focus Publications,
Geanies House, Fearn, Tain, Ross-shire, IV20 1TW,
Scotland, U.K.

Cover design: Daniel van Straaten
Illustrations by Stewart Mingham
Printed and bound in Denmark by Norhaven A/S

All rights reserved. No part of this publication may be reproduced, stored
in a retrieval system, or transmitted, in any form, by any means, electronic,
mechanical, photocopying, recording or otherwise without the prior permission
of the publisher or a licence permitting restricted copying. In the U.K. such
licences are issued by the Copyright Licensing Agency, Saffron House, 6-10
Kirby Street, London, EC1 8TS. www.cla.co.uk

Scripture quotations, unless otherwise indicated, are based on the New King
James Version. Copyright © 1982 by Thomas Nelson, Inc. Used by permission.
All rights reserved.

For Lydia and Esther

Lydia
Now a certain woman named Lydia heard . . .
The Lord opened her heart.
Acts 16: 14

Esther
Who knows whether you have come to the kingdom
for such a time as this?
Esther 4: 14

CONTENTS

CONTENTS

The Right Direction

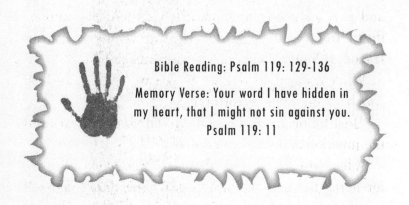

Bible Reading: Psalm 119: 129-136

Memory Verse: Your word I have hidden in my heart, that I might not sin against you.
Psalm 119: 11

H as anyone ever stopped you in the street to ask directions? Sometimes that happens to me. A visitor to the town asks the way to a certain road or perhaps to the Post Office.

Recently we were in America and needed to ask for directions. We had a hired car and wanted to get to another town. Our map book was good but we still needed to stop to ask if we were on the right road. Not everyone was helpful. One person could not understand what we were saying and looked at us blankly. Another man gave us very careless directions. "Oh, yes," he said, "that's just two blocks down the road." After we had gone two blocks, we weren't where we were supposed to be. We were still lost.

Another person gave us a very clear and confident list of instructions. We followed them exactly but then we found that we were headed in completely the wrong direction. Some people, however, were patient and kind and gave us good directions. How grateful we were to them. We eventually got to where we wanted to go and stayed with one of our friends who lives there.

When it was time to go we asked her, "What's the best way back on to the motorway?"

"Just follow me," she said. "I will go in my car until the junction and show you the way."

What an easy journey that was! She wins the prize for being the most helpful person. She didn't just tell us where to go, she showed us! We are all on a journey through life. God has given us his Word, the Bible to direct us on this journey. Just like when you use a map to show you where to go, we should use the Bible to tell us how to behave and what to do.

Sometimes we ask others for help or advice on our journey. How important to ask the right people and not to follow wrong advice. Someone who doesn't know God or the Bible will be of no help. In his first letter, John tells us to "test the spirits whether they are of God, because many false prophets have gone out into the world" (1 John 4: 1). Someone who is careless isn't any help to you. Even someone who is confident and sincere will lead us astray if their advice is wrong. "There is a way that seems right to a man but its end is the way to death" (Proverbs 14: 12).

The advice given by someone who is familiar with the land we are travelling towards – heaven – who is loving, patient and kind is the one who is worth listening to. The best person to listen to is the Lord Jesus himself. He knows heaven well. He has come from there. "Come, follow me," he says. "I will lead you there myself."

REMEMBER TO PRAY

ACTS: A stands for Adoration. (Tell God you love him.)

C stands for Confession. (Tell God you are sorry.)

T stands for Thanks. (We all know what that means.)

S stands for supplication. (Ask God for what you need.)

BIBLE SEARCH

1. Who was given directions to find his brothers at Dothan? Genesis 37: 17

2. Israel (or Jacob) sent his son Judah ahead to direct his way towards which land? Genesis 46: 28

3. Who gave directions for their return journey to the men spying out the land of Canaan? Joshua 2: 16

4. Whose house did Saul ask directions for, when he was out looking for his father's donkeys? 1 Samuel 9: 18

5. Peter and John were given directions to find the house for the Passover feast. Who were they to follow? Luke 22: 10

6. Ananias was given directions to find Saul in Tarsus. In what street was the house? Acts 9: 11

7. Cornelius was given directions to find Simon Peter. Whose house was he in and where was that house? Acts 10: 6

Binoculars

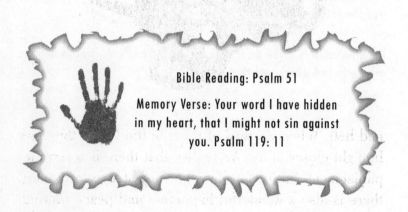

Bible Reading: Psalm 51

Memory Verse: Your word I have hidden in my heart, that I might not sin against you. Psalm 119: 11

Have you ever used a pair of binoculars? We have a small pair of quite powerful ones which we always carry in the car.

Binoculars have several uses. One day we noticed a small black spot in the sky. What could it be? Once we had focused the binoculars we could see it was actually a bird of prey hovering in the sky.

The Bible helps us to see things more clearly too. It points out our sin. It tells us clearly about our need of a Saviour. It tells us all we need to know about the Lord Jesus.

Binoculars help us to see things that are far away and makes them seem closer.

The Bible too tells of things that are far off – things like the judgement seat of Christ and the reality of heaven

and hell. When we read of them in the Bible, they are brought closer to us. We realise that there is a terrible punishment waiting for those who do not love Jesus. But there is also a wonderful happiness and peace waiting for those who do love Jesus.

The captain of a ship uses binoculars to see the dangers that lie ahead – perhaps a reef of rocks or an iceberg.

The Bible warns us of dangers too. On our own, we do not notice the dangers of sin. Lying, stealing or cheating do not seem that bad but the Bible helps us to see that these are sins and that sins are dangerous to our spiritual life. Every sin deserves God's wrath and curse.

Binoculars will help us to find things. Sometimes people go missing on the mountains of Scotland. The Mountain Rescue Team is called out. Part of their equipment will be binoculars which they will use to scan the mountain-sides, hoping to find some sign of the missing person.

The Bible helps us to find happiness through the Lord Jesus Christ. In its pages we find the way of salvation. We learn that the only way to heaven is by trusting in Jesus and what he has done – dying on the cross to pay the price of our salvation.

Next time you use a pair of binoculars, think of how the Bible can help you to get to know Jesus.

REMEMBER TO PRAY

ACTS: Adoration. Confession. Thanks. Supplication.

BIBLE SEARCH

Fill in the missing words. The initial letters spell BINOCULARS.

1. _____ on the Lord Jesus Christ, and you will be saved. Acts 16: 31

2. How shall we escape _____ we neglect so great a salvation. Hebrews 2: 3

3. For with God _____ is impossible. Luke 1: 37

4. By one Man's _____ many will be made righteous. Romans 5: 19

5. Seek the Lord while he may be found, _____ upon him while he is near. Isaiah 55: 6

6. Lord I believe; help my _____ Mark 9: 24

7. The mercy of the _____ is from everlasting to everlasting. Psalm 103: 17

8. I am not _____ of the gospel of Christ, for it is the power of God to salvation for everyone who believes. Romans 1: 16

9. _____ , and believe the gospel. Mark 1: 15

10. Christ Jesus came into the world to save _____ . 1 Timothy 1: 15

The Gift of Books

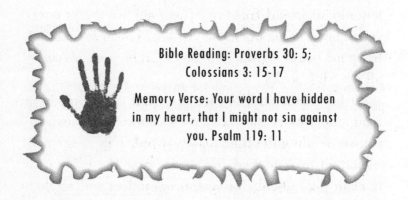

Bible Reading: Proverbs 30: 5;
Colossians 3: 15-17

Memory Verse: Your word I have hidden
in my heart, that I might not sin against
you. Psalm 119: 11

How many books do you have in your house? If your house is like mine, you will have lots. Do you realise that books are a gift from God? Do you use this gift properly?

A few years ago we visited Hong Kong where we met a man who brings Bibles and Christian literature to the Chinese people. He told us with tears in his eyes of how he feels when he visits the Chinese church groups and they ask him, "Have you brought a book for us?" He has never enough books to satisfy the need and sometimes he has to say, "I'm sorry. I have none left."

Christians in China and in many other parts of the world say how wonderful it must be to have such easy access to good books. None of us has to go very far to go to a bookshop or library. How important to make sure we use this gift and do not despise it.

The apostle Paul was keen on books too. When he was in prison in Rome near the end of his life, he wrote a letter to his friend Timothy. "There are two things I need you to bring to me when you visit me. I need my coat and bring my books." Even in prison what he wanted most of all were his books.

In his other letter to Timothy, Paul tells Timothy to read lots. This is good advice for us too. This means, of course, reading the Bible, God's Word. This is the most important book to read. We should read the Bible more than any other book. It is a lamp to our feet and a light to our path. It is where we meet the Saviour, the Lord Jesus Christ. It shows us the way of salvation. We learn how to live in a way that pleases God. We also learn how we should treat other people and how we should behave.

Some people do not yet have a Bible in their own language. Missionaries all over the world are working hard to translate God's Word into different languages.

I heard recently of a man in North Korea who was so keen to have a copy of the Bible that he wrote it all down himself as it was being spoken on a radio programme. How thankful we should be to the Lord for having his Word in our own language and being able to read it. Make sure you read it.

Books are made up of words. The Bible, God's book, is made up of the words of truth. Jesus himself is the Word made flesh, bringing to us God's message of salvation.

REMEMBER TO PRAY

ACTS: Adoration. Confession. Thanks. Supplication.

BIBLE SEARCH

Find the missing words. The initial letters will spell out something that we should take care to do.

1. That night the king could not sleep. So one was commanded to bring the book of the _____ of the chronicles, and they were read before the king. Esther 6: 1

2. Of making many books there is no _____. Ecclesiastes 12: 12

3. The Lord said to Moses, "Whoever has sinned _____ me, I will blot him out of my book." Exodus 32: 33

4. There are also many other things that Jesus _____, which if they were written one by one, I suppose that even the world itself could not contain the books that would be written. John 21: 25

5. You are an epistle of Christ . . . written not with _____ but by the Spirit of the living God. 2 Corinthians 3: 3

6. Jesus said to them, "Yes, have you _____ read, 'out of the mouths of babes . . . you have perfected praise'?" Matthew 21: 16

7. Till I come _____ attention to reading, to exhortation, to doctrine. 1 Timothy 4: 13

Answer _____

Planting the Bulbs

Bible Reading: Isaiah 55: 6-13;
Deuteronomy 11: 18-19.

Memory Verse: Your word I have hidden
in my heart, that I might not sin against
you. Psalm 119: 11

Have you ever planted bulbs in the garden? Each autumn I go to a garden centre to buy some bulbs. They do not look very beautiful, but beside each box of bulbs there is a picture of lovely colourful flowers. There is a marvellous choice of tulips, hyacinths, daffodils and many others.

At home I plant some of the bulbs in a tub at the back door, covering them with soil and giving them a good drink of water. If you were to come to my back door in November and look at the tub, you would not know that there was anything there at all. But I would know that the bulbs were there because I planted them. If you were to come back in the spring, I hope you would then see beautiful spring flowers.

You may sometimes wonder why you should bother to learn verses of the Bible. These Bible verses are like the bulbs – hidden away in your mind – perhaps nobody else knows that they are there. If that knowledge is fed by the "Sun of Righteousness" (that is the Lord Jesus) and by the rain or water of the Holy Spirit, what a difference everybody would see in your life. You would then be able to trust in the Lord Jesus to save you from your sins. The Word of God would be hidden in your mind and would blossom out in your life. People would see that you obey God. A person who obeys God has a beautiful life . . . just like a beautiful flower or blossom.

We recently met a man called Alec. He was brought up in a Christian home. When he grew up he moved to another part of the country and forgot about what his parents had taught him.

As we talked with him we discovered that he knew a minister that we had also known.

"Mr M. used to come to our house often," Alec said. "He once asked me to learn a verse from the Psalms. But he never asked me to repeat it the next time he came back." That had been a bit of a disappointment to him.

"But can you still remember the verse?" he was asked.

"Oh yes, it has never left me."

Then Alec sang the verse to quite a large company of people. "Remember me, O Lord, with the favour which you have toward your people. Oh, visit me with your salvation." (Psalm 106: 4 Scottish Metrical Psalms)

Other memories of sermons heard long ago came flooding back to him – the word that had been hidden away for years began to come back into his memory.

If you plant any bulbs in the autumn, watch out for them coming through the ground. Pray that God would bless His Word to you – even verses that you have already learned – that you would remember them in later years and that they would prove to be a blessing to your soul.

"So shall my word be that goes forth from my mouth; it shall not return to me void, but it shall accomplish what I please, and it shall prosper in the thing for which I sent it." (Isaiah 55: 11)

REMEMBER TO PRAY

ACTS: Adoration. Confession. Thanks. Supplication.

BIBLE SEARCH

Fill in the words missing. The first letters will spell out one of the words in Alec's verse.

1. Now the parable is this: the _____ is the Word of God. Luke 8: 11

2. Put on the whole _____ of God . . . and the sword of the Spirit which is the Word of God. Ephesians 6: 11&17

3. Those who are planted in the house of the _____ shall flourish in the courts of our God. Psalm 92: 13

4. Look down from heaven and see and visit this _____. Psalm 80: 14

5. Restore us, O God of our salvation, and cause your _____ toward us to cease. Psalm 85: 4

6. He shall be like a _____ planted by the rivers of water, that brings forth its fruit in its season. Psalm 1: 3

7. God raised up for _____ a Saviour. Acts 13: 23

8. _____ my eyes that I may see wonderful things from your law. Psalm 119: 18

9. I will offer to you the sacrifice of thanksgiving, and will call upon the _____ of the Lord. Psalm 116: 17

Answer _____

Maker's Instructions

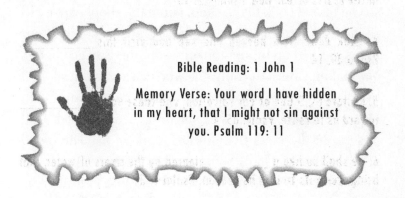

Bible Reading: 1 John 1

Memory Verse: Your word I have hidden in my heart, that I might not sin against you. Psalm 119: 11

We bought a new carpet cleaner in the sales. It had levers to adjust the height, buttons to change the suction, extra fittings for reaching faraway corners. Before we could use it properly we had to read the instruction book. Only then could we make it do what the maker had designed it to do.

If we want to live our lives as God intends us to, we have to study his instruction book – the Bible. If we ignore it things will go wrong as we are not living in the way God wants us to. In the Bible we learn of God's Son, the Lord Jesus, who came to this world to give his life for his people so that they may have life. (John 10: 10).

God's Word teaches us how to please God – trusting him and obeying his commands. It teaches us how to treat our family, friends and even our enemies. We must read the Bible to get the best out of our life.

When something goes wrong with the toaster or kettle, what do you do? Repairing it yourself could be dangerous, so you take it back to the shop. Often the shopkeeper will send it back to the maker to get it repaired. When our life is messed up by sin, the only solution is to go back to our Maker. God is the only one who can sort a life spoiled by sin. We cannot sort it ourselves. No matter how much we try to be good, that will not work. We must ask God to sort out the mess that sin has made of us. The blood of Jesus Christ, God's Son, cleanses us from all sin. "If we confess our sins, he is faithful and just to forgive us our sins and to cleanse us from all unrighteousness." (1 John 1: 9)

Our vacuum cleaner looks very fine but it would not work at all unless it was plugged into a power source. If we love the Lord and trust him we have the power source of God the Holy Spirit to make our life pleasing to God. Make your life the best it can be . . . love Jesus and trust in him. Live to your full potential – obey God's Word.

REMEMBER TO PRAY

ACTS: Adoration. Confession. Thanks. Supplication.

BIBLE SEARCH

Find the missing word in each verse. The initials of your answers will spell out two words connected with the story.

1. God said, "Let us make _____ in our image." Genesis 1: 26

2. The Spirit of God has made me, and the breath of the _____ gives me life. Job 33: 4

3. Let us _____ before the Lord our maker. Psalm 95: 6

4. The day that God created man on the _____. Deuteronomy 4: 32

5. Your _____ hand upholds me. Psalm 63: 8

6. By him all things were created . . . whether thrones or dominions or principalities or _____ . Colossians 1: 16

7. We ought to _____ God rather than men. Acts 5: 29

8. All things were made through him, and _____ him nothing was made that was made. John 1: 3

9. He who believes in me has _____ life. John 6: 47

10. _____ now your Creator in the days of your youth. Ecclesiastes 12: 1

Answer _____   _____

Road Signs

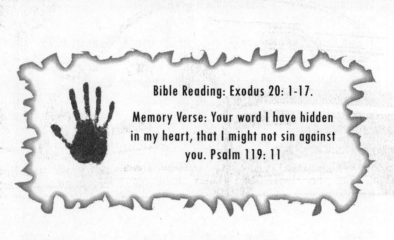

Bible Reading: Exodus 20: 1-17.

Memory Verse: Your word I have hidden in my heart, that I might not sin against you. Psalm 119: 11

Have you got a Highway Code? This is a book which gives you the rules of the road and the meaning of all the road signs. It has been written to help keep road-users safe. If we all drove at any speed or on either side of the road, we would be in a lot of danger. God's Word, the Bible, has been given to us to help us on our journey through life. God's instructions are clear and if we ignore them we are in great danger.

Some signs tell us not to do something – Don't come in here; Don't go any faster; Stop. God in his Word forbids us from doing certain things. "Do not covet." "Do not lie." "Do not take the Lord's name in vain." God has given us many orders to stop doing wicked things. We can only do this with the help of the Holy Spirit.

Other road signs give us instructions about what we should do – e.g. turn left, drive at this speed. God gives us instructions too. "Remember the Sabbath day to keep it holy." "Honour your father and your mother." "Be kind one to another."

Some signs give warnings – e.g. road works, wild animals, steep hill. God gives us loving warnings in the Bible. "Watch and pray that you will not fall into temptation." "Flee the evil desires of youth."

Other signs give information – some tell us the distance to the next town or about a parking place or service station. God's Word gives us useful information – the most important being the way of salvation through Jesus Christ. "By grace you have been saved through faith." (Ephesians 2: 8) God's word also tells us how we are to behave. We are told how to please God, serving him and other people.

All drivers have to keep to the rules of the Highway Code. All God's creatures too should live by his code, the Bible.

REMEMBER TO PRAY

ACTS: Adoration. Confession. Thanks. Supplication.

BIBLE SEARCH

Transport in Bible times was very different from what we have today. Find out from the following verses how people travelled then.

1. In the days of Jael, the highways were deserted and the travellers walked along the _____. Judges 5: 6

2. Rebekah lifted her eyes and when she saw Isaac she dismounted from her _____. Genesis 24: 64

3. Let a royal robe be brought which the king has worn and a _____ on which the king has ridden. Esther 6: 8

4. Then Namaan went with his horses and _____. 2 Kings 5: 9

5. They carried the ark of God on a new _____ from the house of Abinadab. 1 Chronicles 13: 7

6. They brought the _____ and the _____ , laid their clothes on them and set him on them. Matthew 21: 7

7. And finding a _____ sailing over to Phoenicia, we went aboard and set sail. Acts 21: 2

Sowing the Seeds

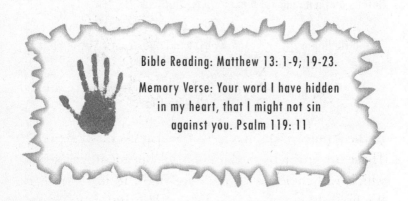

Bible Reading: Matthew 13: 1-9; 19-23.

Memory Verse: Your word I have hidden in my heart, that I might not sin against you. Psalm 119: 11

One day I bought a packet of sunflower seeds. In the one little packet were seventy-five seeds. From that one packet it could be possible to grow seventy-five big sunflowers. The instructions on the back told us when, where and how to plant them and said that each plant could grow as tall as one and a half to three metres high. The picture on the packet looked most impressive and I hoped to have some lovely sunflowers in my garden in the summer months.

However, if you were to keep the seeds in the packet you would not get any flowers. The seeds have to be planted in the ground. They also need plenty of water and the warmth of the sunshine. Only then will they grow and produce sunflowers. If you drive through France

in the summer you may see whole fields of sunflowers. These are grown by the farmer to produce a crop of seeds which will then make sunflower oil. The little seed in the field does not only produce a beautiful flower but a useful crop.

The Word of God is like a little seed. If we keep our Bible, like a closed packet of seeds, in a cupboard or on the shelf, it will not do anything. Owning a Bible is not enough. The Word of God has to be planted in our minds and take root in our hearts and to grow good fruit in our lives. Your life will grow into a life that is pleasing to God . . . a life of obedience to him.

The Psalmist wrote, "I have hidden your Word in my heart, that I might not sin against you," in Psalm 119: 11. What a difference it would make in our lives if God's word was influencing us so much that we hated sin and turned from it. It is good for us to try to memorise God's word and to think about it whenever we can. God the Holy Spirit will bring to our memories the things that we have learned. "The Holy Ghost . . . will teach you all things and bring to your remembrance all things I said to you." (John 14: 26). If the word of God is not already in our mind it cannot be brought back to our memory.

I do not really expect that all seventy-five sunflower seeds in my packet will produce a huge flower.

Jesus tells us in the parable of the sower (Matthew 13) that not all the seeds sown produced good fruit. Some seeds fell on the roadside and the birds ate them; some landed on stony ground and the heat scorched them; some were choked by thorns and weeds.

Not every person who hears the word of God produces spiritual fruit. Not everyone who reads the Bible trusts in God or obeys the instructions there. Satan can stop people trusting in God. He can make them disobey God's Word. Satan can make you care too much about money and clothes, instead you should be caring about God and what he wants. Satan can make you careless about obeying God. He can make you think that God's Word isn't important. We should listen to Jesus' warnings and live our life in a way that is pleasing to him.

REMEMBER TO PRAY

ACTS: Adoration. Confession. Thanks. Supplication.

BIBLE SEARCH

Fill in the missing words and then read Galatians 5.

1. This is _____, that we walk according to his commandments. 2 John: 6

2. These things have I spoken to you, that my _____ may remain in you and that your _____ may be full. John 15: 11

3. And the _____ of God which surpasses all understanding will guard your hearts and minds through Christ Jesus. Philippians 4: 7

4. Convince, rebuke, exhort, with all _____ and teaching. 2 Timothy 4: 2

5. "Is there anyone who is left of the house of Saul, that I may show him _____ for Jonathan's sake." 2 Samuel 9: 1

6. Now I myself am confident concerning you, my brethren, that you are full of _____ filled with all knowledge, able also to admonish one another. Romans 15: 14

7. May the Lord repay every man for his righteousness and his _____. 1 Samuel 26: 23

8. Let your _____ be known to all. Philippians 4: 5

9. Add to your faith virtue; to virtue, knowledge; to knowledge _____ - _____ to _____ - _____ perseverance. 2 Peter 1: 5-6

Faith in Action

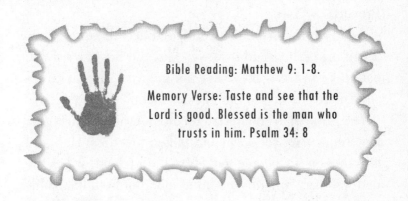

Bible Reading: Matthew 9: 1-8.

Memory Verse: Taste and see that the Lord is good. Blessed is the man who trusts in him. Psalm 34: 8

Recently we went for a walk along a steep mountain path. It was quite difficult. We had to be careful it was good to complete the walk safely and in good time. We met many people on the path, some fit and athletic, others found the walk a great struggle.

We were very impressed by two men we met on the way. One was blind, the other was his friend and guide. The blind man completely trusted his friend who gave instructions and warnings of rocks and difficulties ahead. The blind man put his hand on his guide's shoulder and followed his movements. It reminded us of the trust we should put in the Lord Jesus Christ. Our life is like a journey on a difficult path. Jesus instructs and warns us in his Word. We should obey what he says to us.

He also wants us to trust him to take us safely on our journey. "Trust in the Lord with all your heart and lean not on your own understanding. In all your ways acknowledge him and he shall direct your paths." (Proverbs 3: 5–6).

God has promised his people that he will guide them. "I will bring the blind by a way they did not know. I will lead them in paths they have not known... These things will I do for them and not forsake them." (Isaiah 42: 16)

The blind man and his friend did not walk all the time. Sometimes they sat down and talked together. The Lord does this for his people too. He is their friend. When the road was very difficult the blind man put both his hands on his friend's shoulders instead of just one. When life is very difficult for us, we have to lean all the more on the Lord. "My times are in your hand." (Psalm 31: 15)

REMEMBER TO PRAY

ACTS: Adoration. Confession. Thanks. Supplication.

BIBLE SEARCH

The first letters of the missing words spell out two important words.

1. He will not allow your _____ to be moved; he who keeps you will not slumber. Psalm 121: 3

2. So shall I have an _____ for him who reproaches me: for I trust in your word. Psalms 119: 42.

3. The apostles said to the Lord, "_____ our faith." Luke 17: 5

4. The word of the Lord is proven: he is a shield to all who _____ in him. 2 Samuel 22: 31

5. So then faith comes by _____, and hearing by the word of God. Romans 10: 17

6. My high _____, and my deliverer. Psalm 144: 2

7. The Lord is my _____ and my fortress and my deliverer. 2 Samuel 22: 2

8. But my eyes are _____ you, O God the Lord. Psalm 141: 8

9. I have also trusted in the Lord; I shall not _____. Psalm 26: 1

10. Jesus said to him, "I am the way, the _____ and the life." John 14: 6

Answer _____   _____

Baking a Cake

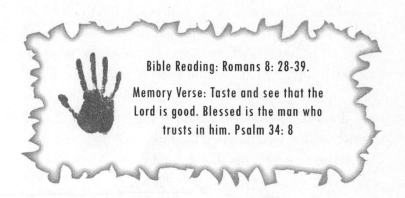

Bible Reading: Romans 8: 28-39.

Memory Verse: Taste and see that the Lord is good. Blessed is the man who trusts in him. Psalm 34: 8

Have you ever baked a cake? You take flour, baking powder, eggs, sugar and margarine, beat them together thoroughly, then bake the mixture in the oven. Delicious! Sugar and eggs taste nice, but have you ever tasted a spoon full of flour? A teaspoonful of baking powder is even worse. But all these ingredients together make a lovely cake and without any one of them the cake would not taste so good.

Our lives are made up of many different experiences. Some of these we find very sweet and pleasant. Others we find unpleasant and difficult – perhaps some sadness or a hard time at school – but God uses all these experiences together to make our lives better and to help us to trust in him. "We know that all things work together for good to those who love God, to those who are called according to his purpose." (Romans 8: 28)

When we think about Joseph's life we see many difficult experiences. He was thrown into a pit by his brothers, he was sold as a slave and put into prison unjustly. He had good experiences too — being made Prime Minister of Egypt, for example. All these experiences were used by God for Joseph's good and the good of his family. Even the evil deeds of his brothers were used by God. Looking back Joseph was able to say to them "You meant evil against me, but God meant it for good." (Genesis 50: 20). The old poem expresses this so well.

"My life is but a weaving,
between my God and me.
I do not choose the colours,
He worketh steadily.
Oft times he weaveth sorrow,
And I in foolish pride,
Forget he sees the upper,
And I the underside.

Not till the loom is silent
And the shuttles cease to fly,
Will God unroll the canvas
And explain the reasons why.
The dark threads are as needful
In the skilful Weaver's hand,
As the threads of gold and silver
In the pattern he has planned."

Just as the baker needs baking powder and flour as well as sugar for a good cake – so God uses the difficult or sad times to make us what he wants us to be.

REMEMBER TO PRAY

ACTS: Adoration. Confession. Thanks. Supplication.

BIBLE SEARCH

I was once given the following recipe for a scripture cake. I have actually made it and it works quite well. Look up the verses to find out the recipe. Use Authorised Version for ingredients.

Ingredients

4.5 cups 1 Kings 4: 22	1.5 cups Judges 5: 25b
2 cups Jeremiah 6: 20	2 cups 1 Samuel 30: 12
2 cups Nahum 3: 12	1 cup Numbers 17: 8
2 tbsp 1 Samuel 14: 25	6 articles Jeremiah 17: 11
A pinch of Leviticus 2: 13	2 tsp Amos 4: 5

Season to taste with 2 Chronicles 9: 9

Method

Bake for one hour in a moderate oven.
Follow Solomon's advice for making a good child –
Proverbs 23: 14, and you have a good cake.

Clothes

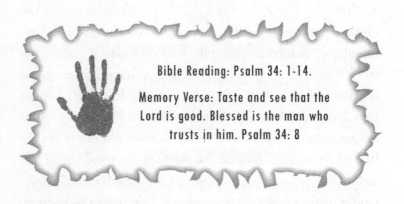

Bible Reading: Psalm 34: 1-14.

Memory Verse: Taste and see that the Lord is good. Blessed is the man who trusts in him. Psalm 34: 8

Most people like to dress smartly for a special occasion like a wedding or a party. This can be quite expensive. Perhaps you like to wear special clothes for playing football or going to the gym. Sports gear can be expensive too. Sometimes it can seem

so important to be dressed properly – but why? Is it just so that other people can admire us? The Bible tells us about the special clothing that a Christian has and what's more it doesn't cost a penny!

Peter in his first letter tells the Christians to "be clothed with humility". (1 Peter 5: 5). Humility is very beautiful. Someone who has humility has a right view of God and of themselves. When you have humility you realise how wicked and sinful you are but you also see how beautiful God is. The person who is proud or self-important does not please God. He does not give God the first place in his life. If we make God the most important and ourselves the least important, we are being humble. God will then exalt us and take us when we die to be in heaven with him.

Isaiah tells us about lovely clothes that God has given to him and every Christian. "For he has clothed me with the garments of salvation, he has covered me with the robe of righteousness, as a bridegroom decks himself with ornaments, and as a bride adorns herself with her jewels." (Isaiah 61: 10).

What an amazing gift! It is a gift for all of us who look to Christ for help and forgiveness of sins. This gift is freely given to all who repent and with grief and hatred of their sin, turn to follow and love the Lord.

The robe of righteousness is a gift from Christ too. "All our righteousnesses are like filthy rags." (Isaiah 64: 6). We may try our best to do what is right but that is not acceptable to God. He wants us to realise that we need to be covered with the righteousness of Christ. "Blessed is he whose transgression is forgiven, whose sin is covered." (Psalm 32: 1).

Paul in his letter to the church at Colosse tells them to be clothed with compassion, kindness, humility, gentleness, patience and especially love. People should see all these things in the life of a Christian. The people of the world who don't love Christ may be critical, mean, proud of themselves, haughty and easily irritated. Christians should not be like that – they should be different. Are we sometimes more like the people of the world than we should be? Ask the Lord to help you to be different. Ask Jesus to make you like him – loving, gentle, kind and patient.

When you are clothed like that you are the best dressed person on earth.

Do you like to buy new clothes and get dressed up? God's word tells us in Proverbs 31 what the best dressed people wear. This chapter tells us about a lady. "She is clothed with strength and dignity; she can laugh at the days to come." What does God mean by strength? He doesn't mean muscles or being able to lift a really heavy weight. The strength that God tells us about here is the strength that we get from trusting in him. When we trust in God he gives us the strength for all the problems and difficulties that we face.

When we have strength from God and are kind to other people this is better than the best sports gear we can buy. When you love God with all your heart and soul and mind, it's far better than that gorgeous dress you saw in the shop window. Having love, mercy, humility and patience will make you really beautiful in God's eyes. God is the only one that really matters. It is his opinion that we should care about. All the beautiful, expensive clothes that we buy in the shops today will soon be worn out, torn, faded or thrown away but the special "clothes" God gives to his people are lasting and always beautiful.

REMEMBER TO PRAY

ACTS: Adoration. Confession. Thanks. Supplication.

BIBLE SEARCH

The initial letters of the missing words spell out a garment that God gives us and which we read about in Proverbs 31.

1. I will also clothe her priests with _____ , and her saints shall shout aloud for joy. Psalm 132: 16

2. If only I may _____ his garment, I shall be made well. Matthew 9: 21

3. I put on _____, and it clothed me; my justice was like a robe and a turban. Job 29: 14

4. Command those who are rich in this present age not to be haughty, nor to trust in uncertain riches but in the living God, who gives us richly all things to _____. 1 Timothy 6: 17

5. I counsel you to buy from me . . . , white garments that you may be clothed, that the shame of your _____ may not be revealed. Revelation 3: 18

6. To console those who mourn in Zion, to give them beauty for ashes, the oil of joy for mourning, the _____ of praise for the spirit of heaviness. Isaiah 61: 3

7. Stand therefore having girded your waist with _____. Ephesians 6: 14

8. The fear of the Lord is the instruction of wisdom, and before _____ is humility. Proverbs 15: 33

Answer _____

Telling Others

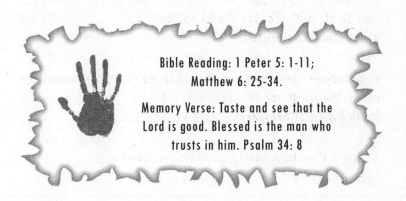

Bible Reading: 1 Peter 5: 1-11;
Matthew 6: 25-34.

Memory Verse: Taste and see that the
Lord is good. Blessed is the man who
trusts in him. Psalm 34: 8

W e have just come back from a holiday on one of
the Canary Islands. We booked it from a travel
brochure and did not really know what to expect.
Just before we left a friend came round to our house with a
couple of maps and some photos. She had been to the same
place a few months before. She gave us tips about what to
go and see and the best place to eat. On our first evening
we wondered where we would go for our meal.

"Marina said that the El Patio restaurant was very
good. We could try it."

So on her personal recommendation we went to the
restaurant and enjoyed a lovely meal.

We might have discovered the restaurant in a tourist
guide or we might have come across it in the passing

but having it personally recommended made us go there with much more confidence. Marina was happy to tell us something that had worked for her and we benefited from it.

Do you tell other people about how wonderful Jesus is? Do you tell your friends about what a great friend Jesus is? Do you tell them about Jesus' salvation, about forgiveness of sins? Do you tell them that they can find out about this in God's Word, the Bible?

The Psalmist urges his friends to taste and see that God is good. He recommends it as something worth trying. Not until we had actually tried the restaurant for ourselves could we truly know how good it was. Not until we actually trust in Jesus Christ for ourselves, do we know what a wonderful Saviour he is.

"There are some wonderful beaches along the south coast. You should try them," she told us. "But the road is really dreadful – far worse than a farm track – very rough."

One day we decided to look for these lovely beaches. We followed the directions on the map – turned off the main road on to cinder track – what a rough road! If we had not been warned about it we would have been sure that we were going the wrong way. But because we had been told that the destination was worth the difficult journey, we kept going. And indeed it was worth it.

We can encourage people to keep going in the Christian life. When we have come through a problem or a difficult time, we can be of help to others facing a similar problem later. Jesus encourages us "In the world you will have tribulation; but be of good cheer, I have overcome the world." (John 16: 33).

REMEMBER TO PRAY

ACTS: Adoration. Confession. Thanks. Supplication.

BIBLE SEARCH

The initials of the missing words spell out three things that Jesus is.

1. This is the way; _____ in it. Isaiah 30: 21

2. If any of you lacks wisdom, let him _____ of God. James 1: 5

3. Remember now your Creator in the days of your _____. Ecclesiastes 12: 1

4. _____ and see that the Lord is good. Psalm 34: 8

5. The goodness of God leads you to _____. Romans 2: 4

6. Trust in the Lord with all your heart: and lean not on your own _____. Proverbs 3: 5

7. The LORD is good, a stronghold in the day of _____.
Nahum 1: 7

8. Moses said to _____ . . . "Come with us and we will treat you well; for the LORD has promised good things to Israel."
Numbers 10: 29

9. Indeed I have given him as a witness to the people, a _____ and a commander for the people. Isaiah 55: 4

10. For with God nothing will be _____.
Luke 1: 37

11. Elijah came to all the people and said, "How long will you falter between two opinions? If the LORD is God, _____ him; but if Baal, follow him." 1 Kings 18: 21

12. "Praise the LORD of hosts, for the LORD is good, for his mercy _____ for ever." Jeremiah 33: 11

Answer _____ _____ _____

Going on a Journey

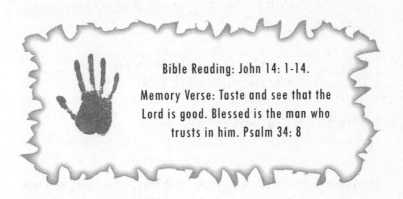

Bible Reading: John 14: 1-14.

Memory Verse: Taste and see that the Lord is good. Blessed is the man who trusts in him. Psalm 34: 8

Have you ever been on a plane? Some people can be very nervous when the plane is taking off or landing. They clutch at the arm rests, and refuse to look out of the window. Others are very confident and relaxed. They are quite sure that the plane will land safely.

Both people are in the same place. The place delivers the nervous person as well as the confident person to the airport. The safety of the journey does not depend on the faith you have in the plane but on the reliability of the plane, the object of the faith.

Faith in God is like that too. The really important part about faith is not how much we have in whom we are putting our faith. Jesus speaks about someone having faith as a grain of mustard seed which is a very tiny seed. If that tiny faith is in the right object – God, then that is all that matters. When you put your faith in God, he will save you from your sins, even if your faith is very little and weak. "For by grace you have been saved through faith." (Ephesians 2: 8).

One godly old lady was complemented one day by a friend. "You are a woman of great faith," she said. "Oh no," replied the old lady, "I am a woman of little faith in a great God."

Another way of illustrating faith is the ice covering a pond in a cold frosty winter. If the ice is thick and strong, it will support someone even if he is walking on it nervously. If the ice is reliable, it will hold him up. If the ice is thin and weak, no matter how confident the man is, it will not hold him up. Great faith in the wrong thing or person is dangerous.

Jesus Christ is truly strong and reliable. He deserves our trust and faith. He will never let us down. He is true. All he says is true. "I am the way, the truth and the life," he says. (John 14: 6) He is the good shepherd who gives his life for his sheep. (John 10: 11) He is the light of the world who is the only sure guide in every situation. (John 8: 12) He is the bread of life who gives us sustenance and nourishment and helps us to grow in grace. (John 6: 48) He is also the resurrection and the life. (John 11: 25) The one who believes in him (or has faith in him) though he were dead, yet shall he live.

What a wonderful Saviour for us to believe in. He that believes in the Son has everlasting life: and he who does not believe the Son shall not see life, but the wrath of God abides on him. (John 3: 36)

REMEMBER TO PRAY

ACTS: Adoration. Confession. Thanks. Supplication.

BIBLE SEARCH

Fill in the gaps. The initial letters spell out the story subject.

1. Stephen, a man _____ of faith and the Holy Spirit. Acts 6: 5

2. Through whom (Jesus) also we have _____ by faith into this grace. Romans 5: 2

3. The apostles said to the Lord, "_____ our faith." Luke 17: 5

4. Faith is the substance of _____ hoped for. Hebrews 11: 1

5. So then faith comes by _____, and hearing by the word of God. Romans 10: 17

6. Jesus said . . . "I say to you, I have not found such great faith, not even in _____." Luke 7: 9

7. And his _____, through faith in his name, has made this man strong. Acts 3: 16

8. For by _____ you have been saved. Ephesians 2: 8

9. To those who have _____ like precious faith with us by the righteousness of our God and Saviour Jesus Christ. 2 Peter 1: 1

10. Thus also faith by itself, if it does not have works, is _____. James 2: 17

Answer _____   _____   _____

Fire Danger

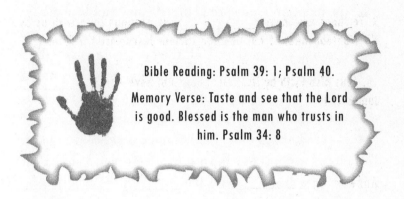

Bible Reading: Psalm 39: 1; Psalm 40.

Memory Verse: Taste and see that the Lord is good. Blessed is the man who trusts in him. Psalm 34: 8

The long hot summer has many effects on the countryside – rivers running low, farm animals short of grass, as well as holiday makers enjoying the sunshine.

Near where we live, there was a moorland fire. The dry heather and moorland vegetation caught fire – perhaps from a carelessly discarded cigarette end or even a spark from a camping stove. The small spark resulted in a lot of damage. Acres of woodland and moorland caught fire. It was a very difficult task for the Fire Brigade. The area is difficult to reach by road and there was not much water in the rivers and lochs to help put out the fire.

God warns us of the danger of careless speech. He compares careless words to a small spark which can do lots of damage. Lies, boasting or telling tales are things we are all guilty of. They displease God and harm others and ourselves.

What we say can spread a great distance. The smoke from the moorland fire spread into the town and set off the hospital smoke alarms. The wind blew powdery ash over the supermarket car park – all the cars were covered.

Our sin has a bad effect on others. A bad example might make someone else sin. A careless word can hurt someone's feelings or make them feel angry.

It is very hard to put a fire out once it gets a firm hold. The moors around our town have deep peaty soil. Peat is used as a fuel in some homes. It burns easily. The Fire Chief said that the moorland fire was burning as deep as three metres down. He said it would possibly go on smouldering for months and would not be put out completely until a heavy fall of snow covered the area.

Our sins, of speech or any other, will continue to burn into our lives until we are covered by the pure righteousness of Christ. The work of Christ is the only effective way of dealing with our sin. We cannot cope with it ourselves – we have no power in ourselves to overcome sin. God has provided the needed rescue for his people. "Blessed is he whose transgression is forgiven, whose sin is covered." (Psalm 32: 1) What a wonderful provision from the Lord for those who put their trust in him – for those who confess their sin. God is faithful and just to forgive their sin and to cleanse them from all unrighteousness.

REMEMBER TO PRAY

ACTS: Adoration. Confession. Thanks. Supplication.

BIBLE SEARCH

Find the missing word from the texts.

1. My tongue also shall _____ of your righteousness all the day long. Psalm 71: 24

2. Gossips and busybodies saying things which they _____ not. 1 Timothy 5: 13

3. They speak idly everyone with his _____. Psalm 12: 2

4. A _____ tongue breaks a bone. Proverbs 25: 15

5. My lips will not speak wickedness nor my tongue _____ deceit. Job 27: 4

6. Keep your tongue from _____. Psalm 34: 13

The initial letters of your answer spell out something found in James chapter 3 which is described as a 'fire, a world of evil', _____.

Precious Jewels

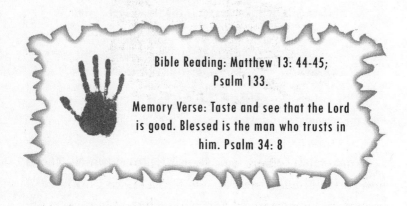

Bible Reading: Matthew 13: 44-45;
Psalm 133.

Memory Verse: Taste and see that the Lord is good. Blessed is the man who trusts in him. Psalm 34: 8

If you look in the window of a jeweller's shop you will notice that diamonds, rubies and emeralds are very expensive. If you own a necklace or a ring, it will be very precious to you and you will take good care of it. God has jewels which are very precious to him. The Bible tells us that each Christian is one of God's jewels. Each one is very precious to him and he will take good care of them. "They shall be like the jewels of a crown." Zechariah 9: 16.

Why are jewels precious? Very hard work is needed to mine jewels from the earth. There are diamond mines in Africa and Australia where tremendous effort is made to extract the jewel-bearing rock. It is difficult and dangerous work.

What great effort was required to produce God's jewels. God had to send his only Son to this world; there he suffered the agony of a cruel death on the cross to pay the price of the sin of each one of his people. This was the hardest work of all but it had to be done to purchase the precious jewels called Christians.

If a jewel is to show its beauty to perfection it needs to be expertly cut. The diamond will then reflect the light and will shine and sparkle.

The Christian needs to be 'cut' in order to shine more brightly and reflect the light of Christ. The cutting is painful. God's word is like a sharp two-edged sword which cuts away at sin.

If a jewel gets dirty it becomes dull. If you take a ring to the jeweller's shop to be cleaned, he will put it into a machine for a short time to be shaken. This treatment cleans the jewel and it shines brightly again.

The Christian needs a shaking sometimes. Very often a problem will shake us out of laziness and make us start praying more. It makes us trust in Jesus Christ. That shaking is good for us.

Jewels are precious because of who owns them. A necklace owned by Queen Victoria would be more valuable than one owned by an unknown person. The Christian is precious because he belongs to Christ. "They were yours; you gave them to me," said Jesus to his Father. What a wonderful comfort to the Christian to know that he belongs to Jesus.

Jewels are more beautiful when they are arranged in a collection. Each stone may have a different colour or shape but together they make an even more beautiful piece of jewellery.

Christians are more beautiful when they are united in love to each other. This unity is pleasing to God.

Jewels are precious because they last. They do not wear out or break. Christ's jewels last too. He has given them eternal life. They shall never perish. These jewels will last even through temptation, problems or difficulties.

REMEMBER TO PRAY

ACTS: Adoration. Confession. Thanks. Supplication.

BIBLE SEARCH

The Christian is described in the Bible as JEWEL. Fill in the missing words from the verses which describe or instruct the Christian.

1. Therefore having been J _____ by faith, we have peace with God through our Lord Jesus Christ. Romans 5: 1

2. Having been justified by his grace we should become heirs according to the hope of E _____ life. Titus 3: 7

3. For we are his W _____ created in Christ Jesus for good works. Ephesians 2: 10

4. Be an E _____ to the believers in word, in conduct, in love, in spirit, in faith and in purity. 1 Timothy 4: 12

5. L _____ one another, as he gave us commandment. 1 John 3: 23

Keep Fit

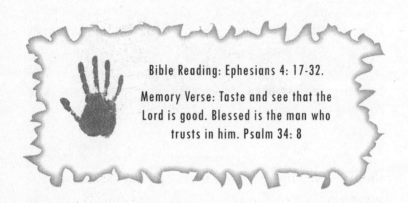

Bible Reading: Ephesians 4: 17-32.

Memory Verse: Taste and see that the Lord is good. Blessed is the man who trusts in him. Psalm 34: 8

It is important to look after our bodies and to keep fit. Lots of books are written about the right food to eat – plenty of fruit and vegetables, not too much sugar and fat. Regular exercise is important too – swimming or walking, taking part in sport or even helping with the housework or gardening. Sleep and rest are also essential for a healthy body.

We are encouraged to look after our bodies by doctors and others. But what about our spiritual fitness? Are we living healthy Christian lives? Are we growing in grace or are our spiritual lives stunted and unhealthy?

Our spiritual lives need good food too. God's word is like nourishing milk which we should long for, so that we may grow (1 Peter 2: 2). We should also read and study

the Bible regularly for our growth in grace. Listening to preaching is also a good way to become strong Christians. Paul told the Colossian Christians that he preached Christ, warning every one and teaching every one so that he might present every one perfect in Christ Jesus.

Prayer can also be used. Paul prayed that his friends would increase in all wisdom and spiritual understanding (Colossians 1: 9). We should have this prayer too for ourselves and for our Christian friends and family.

Our consciences need exercise so that we respond to good and get rid of evil (Hebrews 5: 14). Your conscience is the part of you that feels guilty when you do wrong. It warns you when something is sinful and against God. When you listen to your conscience telling you to be good instead of wicked you are becoming a stronger Christian. Sometimes it is hard to obey and life is difficult. This is a test. If you keep going, you will pass the test. God will make you a more patient person. You will grow up and every day become more like Jesus. Remember that the rest and peace we need is only found in the Lord. "Rest in the Lord and wait patiently for him" (Psalm 37: 7).

What a lot of time we spend feeding, exercising and resting our bodies. How much time do we spend looking after our souls? A strong growing Christian will become more useful to Jesus Christ and will be ready to do good work for him.

REMEMBER TO PRAY

ACTS: Adoration. Confession. Thanks. Supplication.

BIBLE SEARCH

Find the missing words. Clue — the answers spell out KEEP FIT.

1. Grow in the grace and _____ of our Lord and Saviour Jesus Christ. 2 Peter 3: 18

2. That you may walk worthy of the Lord, fully pleasing him, being fruitful in _____ good work. Colossians 1: 10

3. Honour your father and mother . . . that it may be well with you and you may live long on the _____. Ephesians 6: 2-3

4. Filled with the fruits of righteousness which are by Jesus Christ — to the glory and _____ of God. Philippians 1: 11

5. Add to your _____ virtue, to virtue knowledge. 2 Peter 1: 5

6. The apostles said to the Lord "_____ our faith." Luke 17: 5

7. Speaking the _____ in love, may grow up in all things into him who is the Head — Christ. Ephesians 4: 15

Pass the Salt

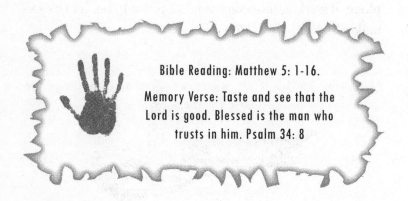

Bible Reading: Matthew 5: 1-16.

Memory Verse: Taste and see that the Lord is good. Blessed is the man who trusts in him. Psalm 34: 8

Salt is probably found in every kitchen. We use it to improve the flavour of our food. If we forget to put salt on the potatoes, then the taste is not so good.

Before the days of freezers, fridges and canned food, salt was used as a preservative. In hot countries meat was well salted and that stopped it from going bad. My grandmother used to put herrings into a barrel with lots of salt. The salt preserved the fish and they could be used weeks and even months later.

Christians are to be like salt in the world because the Christian should have a good effect on the community, whether that is school, college, work or where we live. Perhaps a Christian will stop someone from using bad language. Perhaps they will stop someone from sinning.

In this way Christians can stop the town they live in from becoming worse. The conversation of a Christian can encourage someone else to think of the Lord Jesus or to live in a more God-honouring way. Their school or place of work will become a nicer place to be, just as salt makes food nicer to eat.

Hundreds of years ago salt was used to clean things. In Ezekiel we read about new born babies being rubbed with salt to clean them and to prevent infection. Our daughter had to get four wisdom teeth taken out. The dentist gave her strict instructions to wash her mouth out after every meal with a solution of salt and water until the gums had healed. This was to stop infection.

How can a Christian be like salt in this way? If we live our lives according to God's law and show love and compassion to our friends and neighbours, this may help to have a cleansing influence on the community. Only God can cleanse our hearts and change lives but perhaps our lives can help to lead people to come to Christ for cleansing.

If you ever have a small cut on your finger, and unexpectedly touch salt, how sore it feels. It almost brings tears to your eyes.

If we are to be really like salt, we have to tell people a message from God that may be hard or hurtful. Being told that you are lost and sinful can hurt. Being warned about hell is very hard. If that hurting drives the person to Jesus for healing then it does a lot of good.

Salt is not doing any good if it is still in the packet or in the salt cellar. It has to be used to do good. The Christian too has to be in contact with people if he or she is going to obey Jesus and be like salt in the world.

REMEMBER TO PRAY

ACTS: Adoration. Confession. Thanks. Supplication.

BIBLE SEARCH

1. Who was turned into a pillar of salt because she looked back to the sinful city of Sodom? Genesis 19: 26

2. Which city was known as the city of Salt? Joshua 15: 62

3. Which offering in the Old Testament had to be seasoned with salt? Leviticus 2: 13

4. What did Elisha heal by putting salt in it? 2 Kings 2: 21

5. What did Job think was better eaten with salt? Job 6: 6

6. What is salt good for if it loses its savour or salty taste? Matthew 5: 13

7. What does Paul tell us should always be full of grace, seasoned with salt? Colossians 4: 6

8. What cannot yield both salt and fresh water? James 3: 12

Sing to the Lord

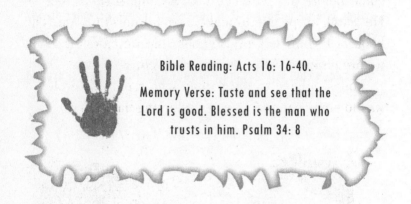

Bible Reading: Acts 16: 16-40.

Memory Verse: Taste and see that the Lord is good. Blessed is the man who trusts in him. Psalm 34: 8

Lying in bed one morning I could hear the marvellous sound of the birds singing with full-throated enthusiasm. It sounded so cheerful and was a reminder that spring was here.

The Bible tells us that the "time of singing" (Song of Solomon 2: 11-12) is a sign that the winter is past.

God cares for the birds. Not even one sparrow falls to the ground without his knowledge. Have you ever heard a blackbird high up on a branch, pouring out its beautiful song which seems like a hymn of praise to its Creator.

How much more reason do we have to sing praises to our Creator. Not only has he made us but he has given his only Son to die for his people on the cross, to save them from the awful misery of hell and to bring them at last to heaven to be with himself.

God commands us to serve him with gladness and to come before his presence with singing (Psalm 100: 2). He wants all people to make a joyful noise to him. The book of Psalms is a praise book that we can sing when we are happy or when we are troubled.

James' advice to the people who received his letter was to sing psalms if they were feeling happy.

Paul and Silas were in prison with their feet fastened in the stocks. At midnight they prayed and sang praises to God in these difficult circumstances (Acts 16).

King Jehoshaphat was being attacked by the people of Moab, Ammon and Mount Seir. He prayed to God for help and guidance. One important part of the battle plan was to appoint a choir who would praise the beauty of the Lord's holiness as they went out before the army

(2 Chronicles 20: 21). Their song was "Praise the Lord, for his mercy endures for ever" (Psalm 136). As they praised the Lord the enemy was defeated.

The saints of God in heaven sing too. John in the book of Revelation tells us that he saw them in his vision singing the song of Moses and the song of the Lamb. "Who shall not fear you, O Lord, and glorify your name? For you alone are holy; for all nations shall come and worship before you; for your judgements have been made manifest" (Revelation 15: 3-4).

So when you hear the birds singing remember to sing songs of praise to God. If we trust in the Lord Jesus as our Saviour our singing becomes new. God, who is so kind and generous, gives us a new song in our heart.

REMEMBER TO PRAY

ACTS: Adoration. Confession. Thanks. Supplication.

BIBLE SEARCH

Find the missing words. The initial letters spell out SING PRAISE.

1. He has put a new _____ in my mouth. Psalm 40: 3

2. The Levites and the priests praised the LORD day by day, singing to the LORD accompanied by loud _____ .
2 Chronicles 30: 21

3. The people could not discern the _____ of the shout of joy from the noise of the weeping of the people. Ezra 3: 13

4. Singing with _____ in your hearts to the Lord. Colossians 3: 16

5. And David and all Israel _____ music before God with all their might and with singing. 1 Chronicles 13: 8

6. It shall blossom abundantly and _____. Isaiah 35: 2

7. Sing _____ to God our strength. Psalm 81: 1

8. Let the _____ of Sela sing. Isaiah 42: 11

9. Let the _____ be joyful in glory. Psalm 149: 5

10. So the ransomed of the LORD shall return, and come to Zion with singing, with _____ joy on their heads. Isaiah 51: 11

The Ploughing Match

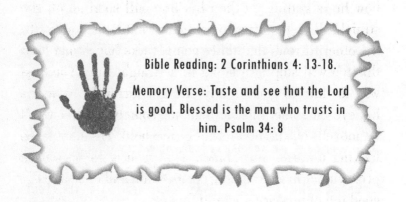

Bible Reading: 2 Corinthians 4: 13-18.

Memory Verse: Taste and see that the Lord is good. Blessed is the man who trusts in him. Psalm 34: 8

Before the farmer sows the seed in his field, he has to prepare the ground. The first thing he does is to plough up the earth with a huge machine made of steel, which turns over the soil to break it up. This is done nowadays with a tractor pulling a plough which may turn over four or six furrows at once. A furrow is the name given to the thin lines you see in the field once it has been ploughed. In the past a single plough was guided by the ploughman and pulled by a horse. It was and still is important that the furrow is as straight as possible.

Ploughing is an important part of the farmer's work but some people enjoy ploughing so much and are so good at it that they enter into special competitions called ploughing matches. The aim of the competition is not to see who can plough the furrow the fastest but to find out who can plough in the straightest line.

If the ploughman keeps looking behind him to see how he is getting on then his line will soon go off the straight. If he just tries to compare what he is doing with the other furrows that other competitors have done then this too will stop him going in a straight line. The best way for him to get a really straight furrow is by fixing his eye on something permanent (something that won't be moved) on the other side of the field. He must keep looking towards that object. That is how to become a prizewinner in a ploughing competition and to do a really good job of preparing a field for seed.

The Christian life is something like a ploughing competition. If we live our lives just looking at ourselves and how we are doing we will soon stray from the right path. If all we do is compare our life to that of our neighbour or friend, then that too will result in us falling into sin.

We ought to live with our eyes fixed firmly on the only permanent, unchanging object of our faith – the Lord Jesus Christ. True blessing is found by living in a way that pleases God. We must look to Jesus, the author and finisher of our faith, who for the joy that was set before him endured the cross, despising the shame, and has sat down at the right hand of the throne of God (Hebrews 12: 2).

When our eyes are fixed firmly on the Lord Jesus, when we are thinking about him and all that he did for his people, what an encouragement that is for us. When we think about Jesus, this encourages us and stops us from being tired and depressed. "Lest you become weary and discouraged in your souls" (Hebrews 12: 3).

So if we feel sad and upset, or feel like giving up, then the answer to that problem is not looking at ourselves, or at our neighbour but looking to the Lord Jesus. We should think about what we read in his Word and about all the things he suffered for his people. He has given us many wonderful promises to encourage us.

REMEMBER TO PRAY

ACTS: Adoration. Confession. Thanks. Supplication.

BIBLE SEARCH

The Bible speaks about ploughing and ploughmen in several places. Find the missing words from the following verses. The initial letters of your answers spell out the word PLOUGH.

1. _____ for war . . . Let all the men of war draw near . . . Beat your ploughshares into swords. Joel 3: 9-10

2. No one having put his hand to the plough and _____ back is fit for the kingdom of God. Luke 9: 62

3. You shall not plough with an ____ and a donkey together. Deuteronomy 22: 10

4. Do not be _____ yoked together with unbelievers. 2 Corinthians 6: 14

5. The days are coming, says the LORD, when the ploughman shall overtake the reaper, and the treader of _____ him who sows seed. Amos 9: 13

6. He who ploughs should plough in _____. 1 Corinthians 9: 10

Dangerous Weapon

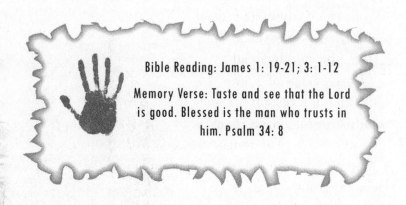

Bible Reading: James 1: 19-21; 3: 1-12

Memory Verse: Taste and see that the Lord is good. Blessed is the man who trusts in him. Psalm 34: 8

You have a very dangerous weapon and so do I. "Not me!" you may be saying. "I don't have a gun or a sword. I wouldn't dream of carrying around something that would hurt anyone." But you do. Mostly it is hidden in a cage behind white bars! Still it can do damage. What am I talking about? Your tongue.

God in his word, tells us that the tongue is evil. What damage and hurt it can do. It can say things that are cruel and hurtful; the tongue can tell lies; your tongue can say things to make you look important and another person stupid. It can do a lot of wicked things. The tongue can say words about God that are not right or say them in a wrong way. God tells us that we should not take his name in vain. We should not use it lightly or irreverently.

We should use it respectfully and honourably. The Lord hates a lying tongue (Proverbs 6: 17). What trouble people have when they bear a false witness or tell lies. Just remember Ananias and Sapphira – they told a lie about what they had done with their possessions. They were punished by death.

In the book of James, we read that the person who can control his tongue can control his whole life. The tongue is compared to the bit in the horse's mouth – it is only very small but it can control the movement of a big horse.

The tongue is also compared to the rudder of a ship – it is very small too but when it is moved by the captain, it can direct a huge ship.

The tongue can have an influence for good. A word of encouragement can make all the difference. Telling the truth in love and praising the Lord are good things that our tongue can do with God's help.

The tongue is also like a little fire that spreads. Many great forest fires have been started with one small match being dropped carelessly. The resulting damage can be immense. Similarly one careless word can cause immense damage and hurt.

Our tongue is described as an unruly evil, full of deadly poison.

David the Psalmist was aware of how dangerous his tongue could be. His prayer was "Set a guard, O Lord, over my mouth; keep watch over the door of my lips" (Psalm 141: 3).

We should make that our prayer too. We should ask the Lord to give us the grace to use our tongues in a way that would please him.

Make this your prayer today – "Keep the door of my lips."

REMEMBER TO PRAY

ACTS: Adoration. Confession. Thanks. Supplication.

BIBLE SEARCH

Find the missing words. The initials will spell out a word which describes the tongue.

1. There is no faithfulness in their mouth; their inward part is
_____. Psalm 5: 9

2. Who sharpen their tongue like a sword, and bend their bows to shoot their _____ – bitter words. Psalm 64: 3

3. But ____ man can tame the tongue. James 3: 8

4. The words of the wise are like _____. Ecclesiastes 12:11

5. The truthful lip shall be _____ for ever. Proverbs 12: 19

6. . . . he (Moses) spoke _____ with his lips. Psalm 106: 33

7. His mouth is full of cursing and deceit and _____ Psalm 10: 7

8. Because I am a man of _____ lips. Isaiah 6: 5

9. Let the lying lips be put to _____. Psalm 31: 18

Answer _____

Real Treasure

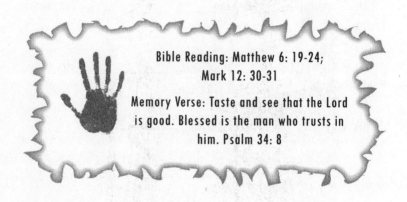

Bible Reading: Matthew 6: 19-24;
Mark 12: 30-31

Memory Verse: Taste and see that the Lord
is good. Blessed is the man who trusts in
him. Psalm 34: 8

Our garage is full of an assortment of items like garden tools, barbecue equipment, toys, games. Some things we use often and other things we keep just in case we find a use for them some day. The other day my grown-up daughter noticed the little two wheeler bicycle that she used to love so much, lying at the back of the garage all rusty. That little bike used to be such a treasure but not any more. Now it is heading for the rubbish dump.

I am sure you like it when Mum and Dad get a new car. It looks so good when it is all shiny and new. But as the years pass scratches and spots of rust appear. Dad can touch them up with new paint but soon the rust comes through again.

The washing machine works well for a few years then it breaks down. To repair the machine can cost more than to buy a new one so the old machine is thrown out.

Whatever possession we have it will probably get broken, rusty, worn out, moth-eaten or even stolen. None of our material goods is of lasting value.

Jesus warns us about this in the Sermon on the Mount in Matthew 6: 19-21.

"Do not lay up for yourselves treasures on earth, where moth and rust destroy and where thieves break in and steal. But lay up for yourselves treasures in heaven where neither moth nor rust destroys and where thieves do not break in and steal. For where your treasure is, there your heart will be also."

Where is our treasure? What do we value most? Is it something which perishes like a car, bike, clothes, a toy or a computer – all soon on the scrap heap? A visit to the town rubbish dump shows how short-lived much of our treasure is.

Treasure in heaven is of lasting value. It will not perish. It is much more important.

How do we get treasure in heaven? We cannot buy it.

Jesus makes us co-heirs of the eternal inheritance which is more valuable than any palace which is more valuable than any palace or estate in this world. God keeps it for us safe and sure.

Do we love God more than earthly things? Do we spend more time and effort in the things of God? If so our treasure is in heaven.

Jesus once met a rich man who asked him how he could inherit eternal life. Jesus told him first about the commandments which the rich young man said he had kept. Jesus then focused on the man's weak spot. "Go and sell what you have and give to the poor. Then you shall have treasure in heaven: and come and follow me" Matthew 19: 21.

The man did not do that. He went away sorrowfully. His sin was, not that he had possessions, but that he loved them more than he loved God.

If we love God and the things of God with the help of the Lord Jesus Christ, then we will have treasures in heaven.

REMEMBER TO PRAY

ACTS: Adoration. Confession. Thanks. Supplication.

BIBLE SEARCH

Find the missing words from the verses. The initial letters will spell out the word TREASURE.

1. Command those who are rich in this present age, not to be haughty, nor to _____ in uncertain riches . . . 1 Timothy 6: 17

2. If _____ increase do not set your heart on them. Psalm 62: 10

3. How hard it is for those who have riches to _____ into the kingdom of God. Mark 10: 23

4. Sell what you have and give _____; provide yourselves money bags which do not grow old, a treasure in the heavens that does not fail . . . Luke 12: 33

5. Jesus said to him, "If you want to be perfect, go _____ what you have and give to the poor, and you will have treasure in heaven." Matthew 19: 21

6. An inheritance incorruptible and _____ and that does not fade away, reserved in heaven for you. 1 Peter 1: 4

7. Trust . . . in the living God who gives us _____ all things to enjoy. 1 Timothy 6: 17

8. Riches certainly make themselves wings; they fly away like an _____ toward heaven. Proverbs 23: 5

Tell the Truth

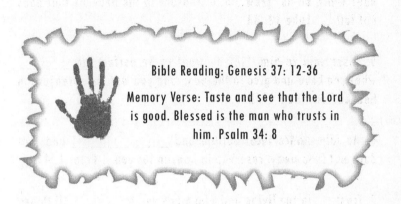

Bible Reading: Genesis 37: 12-36

Memory Verse: Taste and see that the Lord is good. Blessed is the man who trusts in him. Psalm 34: 8

When someone lies to you it destroys your trust in that person. When we lie we may want to cover up something we did wrong, or exaggerate our achievements so that our friends will be impressed. This is wrong because God tells us that is wrong. God tells us "Each of you must put off falsehood and speak truthfully to his neighbour, The Lord detests lying lips, but he delights in men who are truthful."

The ninth commandment says, "You shall not bear false witness against your neighbour" – do not tell lies. The first lie was when the serpent deceived Eve into thinking it would not harm her to eat the forbidden fruit. This led to a lot of trouble for all mankind.

Cain murdered his brother Abel in a fit of jealousy. When God asked him where Abel was, Cain lied. But God knew the truth anyway. Lying did not help him.

Joseph's brothers sold him as a slave. They showed his coat to their father. It had been dipped in animal blood. Jacob thought he had been killed by a wild animal. The brothers had not said it in words, but it was still a lie.

We must ask the Lord to help us to obey this commandment. The Lord Jesus described himself as – the truth. "I am the way, the truth, and the life. No one comes to the Father except through Me" (John 14:6).

Only through him can people "put off falsehood and speak truthfully."

REMEMBER TO PRAY

ACTS: Adoration. Confession. Thanks. Supplication.

BIBLE SEARCH

Find the missing words. The initial letters of your answers will spell out the subject of the chapter.

1. Lying lips are an abomination to the Lord but those who deal
_____ – are his delight. Proverbs 12: 22

2. (They) perish because they did not _____ the love of the truth that they might be saved. 2 Thessalonians 2: 10

3. A false witness will not go _____ and he who speaks lies will not escape. Proverbs 19: 5

4. The truthful lips shall be established for ever, but a lying _____ is but for a moment. Proverbs 12: 19

5. The tongue of the wise promotes _____ Proverbs 12: 18

6. The Word became _____ and dwelt among us and we beheld his glory, the glory as of the only begotten of the Father, full of grace and truth. John 1: 14

7. But the cowardly, _____, abominable murderers . . . and all liars, - shall have their part in the lake which burns with fire and brimstone. Revelation 21: 8

8. Jesus said to him, "I am the way and the truth and the _____. No one comes to the Father except through me." John 14: 6

9. Speak each man the truth to his _____. Zechariah 8: 16

10. Who made heaven and _____, the sea and all that is in them, who keeps truth for ever. Psalm 146: 6

11. Buy the truth and do not _____ it, also wisdom, and instruction and understanding. Proverbs 23: 23

12. But Peter said, "Ananias, why has _____ filled your heart to lie to the Holy Spirit and keep back part of the price of the land for yourself?" Acts 5: 3

Walking in the Way

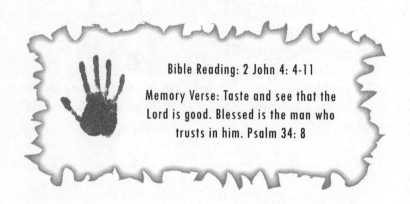

Bible Reading: 2 John 4: 4-11

Memory Verse: Taste and see that the
Lord is good. Blessed is the man who
trusts in him. Psalm 34: 8

Do you remember learning to walk? Probably not. But you did have to learn that very complicated skill.

My little granddaughter has just learned how to walk. Progress is slow. Gradually she has gone from shuffling, to crawling, to standing against the furniture, to standing alone, to at last taking her first step.

Many times she falls down or sits down suddenly. But then she gets up and tries again.

With the helping hand of Mum or Dad, she makes much quicker progress. Just having a finger to hold on to gives her much more confidence. She keeps working at the task; the smile on her face shows how much pleasure she gets from having learnt her new skill of walking.

The Christian life is sometimes described as a walk. "Blessed are those who keep his (God's) testimonies, who seek him with the whole heart! They also do no iniquity: they walk in his ways." (Psalm 119: 2-3)

Starting out in the Christian life is like learning to walk. When a person is converted and turns from serving sin to serving the Lord he starts out on a new way of life – just like a baby's first wobbly steps.

But progress should be made. The believer grows in grace and in the knowledge of the Lord and Saviour Jesus Christ.

Sometimes the Christian tumbles down when he makes a mistake or falls into sin. But just as the loving mum or dad picks up the little child and sets him on his feet again, so the Lord lifts up the fallen believer and restores him to the right way. David prayed after he had fallen into sin. "Restore to me the joy of your salvation." (Psalm 51: 12). We can pray this prayer too.

Just as the mother's hand is such a help to the unsteady toddler, so the strong hand of the Lord and his power is a help to the Christian in his walk. Without Jesus' help, we would fall so many times. When we try to do things in our own strength, we sin and make mistakes.

Just as the baby keeps going and persists in the task of learning to walk, the believer has to keep going in the Christian walk. A Christian has to practice at being patient. He must not give up at the first setback or difficulty. God requires us to be like the good seed (in the story Jesus told) and have fruitful lives – not to be like the seed which fell on the rock, which seemed promising and then withered when things got difficult. A fruitful life is a life that is obedient to God. It pleases him and shows other people how wonderful God is.

The pleasure and happiness of the baby when he finally accomplishes the skill of walking is obvious on his face.

Walking with God and obeying him is the only way to obtain true pleasure. The pleasures of this world are just like grovelling or crawling along the ground.

True blessedness or happiness comes from walking in the law of the Lord, (Psalm 119: 1) trusting in him and leaning on him.

REMEMBER TO PRAY

ACTS: Adoration. Confession. Thanks. Supplication.

BIBLE SEARCH

We are given instructions in God's word as to how we should "walk" the Christian life. Fill in the missing words.

1. Let us walk in the _____ of the Lord. Isaiah 2: 5

2. This is love, that we walk according to his _____.
2 John: 6

3. Blessed is everyone who fears the Lord; who walks in his _____.
Psalm 128: 1

4. What does the Lord require of you but to do justly, and to love mercy and to walk _____ with your God. Micah 6: 8

5. He who walks in his _____ fears the Lord.
Proverbs 14: 2

6. Teach me your way O Lord: I will walk in your _____.
Psalm 86: 11

7. What you are doing is not good. Should you not walk in the _____ of our God. Nehemiah 5: 9

8. He who walks in a _____ way, he shall serve me.
Psalm 101: 6

Trusting in Him

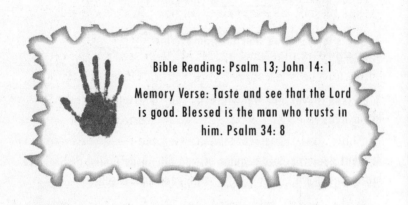

Bible Reading: Psalm 13; John 14: 1

Memory Verse: Taste and see that the Lord is good. Blessed is the man who trusts in him. Psalm 34: 8

The car windscreen was frosted up. Before setting off on our journey, my husband who was driving, quickly scraped a clear space so that he could see where to go.

The windscreen in front of my passenger seat was not as clear so when we were driving along I could not see the road very well.

"Oh, be careful. Can you see where you're going?" I asked nervously.

"Don't worry," was the reply, "I can see fine."

So I had to trust in the driver – his view was better than mine. He could see clearly.

The Lord Jesus can see our circumstances so much better than we can. His view of our life is perfect and complete, whereas we have a view that is only partial. Our weakness, our inability and our sin all blur our vision and cause us to worry about where we are going and what we are doing. But if we place our trust firmly in the Lord Jesus he will take us safely on our life's journey.

"Trust in the Lord with all your heart; and lean not on your own understanding; in all your ways acknowledge him, and he shall direct your paths" (Proverbs 3: 5-6).

Eventually the windscreen in my side cleared up too. I could see clearly where we were going.

The Lord Jesus wants us to be able to see too. He told Paul to go to preach to people who hadn't heard the good news about Jesus Christ so that these people would also see the beauty and wonder of the Lord Jesus himself. The Lord in his Word gives us enlightenment so that we can " . . . know what is the hope of his calling, what are the riches of the glory of his inheritance in the saints" (Ephesians 1: 18).

What a great view to get. What a difference to our lives if we lived committed to the calling of God, looking forward to being with him in glory and trusting in his wonderful power.

David, in the book of Psalms, speaks a lot about trusting in the Lord.

REMEMBER TO PRAY

ACTS: Adoration. Confession. Thanks. Supplication.

BIBLE SEARCH

Find the missing words from the Psalms. The answers spell out our responsibility to God.

1. _____ in him at all times, you people. Psalm 62: 8

2. He is my _____ and my fortress, my God, in him I trust. Psalm 91: 2

3. And _____ his wings you shall take refuge. Psalm 91: 4

4. He will not be afraid of evil tidings; his heart is _____ trusting in the Lord. Psalm 112: 7

5. My heart _____ in him and I am helped. Psalm 28: 7

6. But as for me I trust in you ___ Lord. Psalm 31: 14

7. _____ is the man who trusts in you. Psalm 84: 12

8. Wait silently for God alone, for my _____ is from him. Psalm 62: 5

9. And those who know _____ name will put their trust in you. Psalm 9: 10

Answer _____ _____

A New House

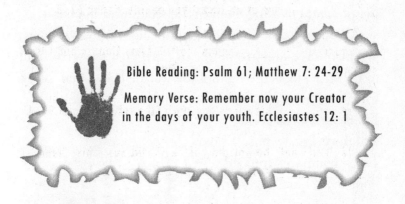

Bible Reading: Psalm 61; Matthew 7: 24-29

Memory Verse: Remember now your Creator in the days of your youth. Ecclesiastes 12: 1

If your family was going to move house you would read through the newspapers to see what was available. The adverts tell you where the house is, how many rooms it has and how much it costs. What suits one family may not suit another. But some things are always necessary. Every house needs a solid foundation and sometimes the builder has to dig down deep to reach firm rock. Jesus spoke in his sermon on the mount about the wise man building his house on the rock. He compared that man to the person who heard God's Word and obeyed it.

Jesus Christ is called the Rock – the firm foundation on whom we should build our lives. If you trust and obey him, he is your strong foundation. You can depend on him.

Every house needs a strong watertight roof and thick walls to protect the family from the cold and rain and danger. God has promised to be the protection for his people. He speaks about being like a wall of fire round his people and covering them in the shadow of his hand.

A house needs windows to allow light into the rooms. We also have electric power in our houses to give light at night. Jesus is the light of the world. Those that follow him shall not walk in darkness but have the light of life. Everyone needs Jesus.

Every house has a door. Jesus compares himself to a door too. "I am the door," he said, "by me if any man enter in, he shall be saved." He is the only way of access into God's kingdom. While we are in this life, God's mercy is offered to us – the door is always open – but if we reject him when we die, the door will be shut for ever.

Some houses have paths leading to the door. Jesus is like a path too. "I am the way," he tells us. "No one comes to the Father except by me." The only way to get to God and heaven is through trusting in Jesus Christ.

If we buy a new house we want it to have good foundations, strong walls and a roof, good windows, a fine door and a clear path. How important it is to make sure that we have Jesus in our lives as the good foundation, as the protection from all evil and sin as the light of our life and as the way of access to God the Father. And what is more this wonderful provision is absolutely free – no cost to us because Jesus has paid it all when he died for his people on the cross at Calvary.

REMEMBER TO PRAY

ACTS: Adoration. Confession. Thanks. Supplication.

BIBLE SEARCH

The missing words are all parts of a house. Can you find them?

1. When they could not come near him because of the crowd, they uncovered the _____ where he was . . . and they let down the bed Mark 2: 4

2. And in a _____ sat a certain young man named Eutychus who was sinking into a deep sleep. Acts 20: 9

3. Then the disciples took him by night and let him down through the _____ in a large basket. Acts 9: 25

4. Now Peter continued knocking and when they opened the _____ and saw him they were astonished. Acts 12: 16

5. You shall write them (God's words) on the _____
of your house and on your _____. Deuteronomy 6: 9

6. Then he will show you a large furnished upper _____ , there
make ready. Luke 22: 12

7. Then the same Sheshbazzar came and laid the
_____ of the house of God which is in Jerusalem.
Ezra 5: 16

8. But Jehoshabeath the daughter of the king took Joash . . . and put
him and his nurse in a _____. 2 Chronicles 22: 11

A New Baby

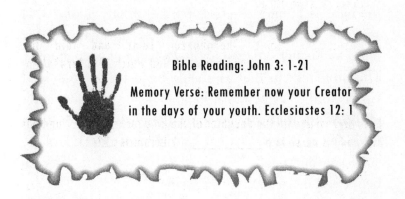

Bible Reading: John 3: 1-21

Memory Verse: Remember now your Creator in the days of your youth. Ecclesiastes 12: 1

Have you ever seen a very young baby? Perhaps you have a little brother or sister. We cannot remember what it was like to be a baby but we have all experienced it. A baby granddaughter, Lydia, has been born in our family recently so we are being reminded of the needs and activities of a newborn baby.

Jesus compared coming to trust in him for salvation to the birth of a baby. "You must be born again," he said to Nicodemus. "No one can see the kingdom of God unless he is born again" (John 3: 3–7).

Crying loudly is one of the first signs of life that a baby shows. One of the first signs of being born again is the cry of prayer to God. When Paul was converted to Christ, he began to pray. Ananias was sent by God to help him. "Go and ask for a man called Saul," he was told, "he is praying." If you pray regularly this is a sign of new life in God.

A baby needs milk for health and growth. When the baby is hungry she does not lie quietly hoping that someone will remember to feed her. She makes a big noise and is not satisfied until she has had enough milk. The Bible tells us that we should be just as keen to read God's word. "As newborn babies, desire the pure milk of the Word, that you may grow thereby" (1 Peter 2: 2). God's Word is the spiritual nourishment that is exactly suited to our needs. We need God's Word to become better and more mature Christians.

The baby has to be washed. She can't do it herself. We need to be washed clean from the dirt of sin. We can't do that ourselves. Only God can clean us from sin through the death of Jesus Christ. "The blood of Jesus, his Son, cleanses us from all sin" (1 John 1: 7).

The little baby is completely dependent on her mother and father. She trusts them to look after her. They will protect her and guide her and correct her too. She learns to love them through the love shown to her. If we love the Lord, it is only because he has first loved us. We are dependent on him for everything – even for the breath we draw. If we trust in the Lord with all our heart and acknowledge him in all our ways, he has promised to direct our lives (Proverbs 3).

A mother loves her little baby so much. God tells us that his love for his people is even greater. "Can a mother forget the baby at her breast? Though she may forget, I will not forget you."

REMEMBER TO PRAY

ACTS: Adoration. Confession. Thanks. Supplication.

BIBLE SEARCH

1. Who was the first baby born into the world? Genesis 4

2. Which baby was hidden from danger in the River Nile? Exodus 2

3. Who was the mother who prayed for a baby in the temple in Shiloh? 1 Samuel 1

4. Who was the baby whose father was struck dumb? Luke 1

5. Whose birth was announced by the angels to the shepherds? Luke 2

6. Which baby was born when his father was 100 years old? Genesis 21

7. Which baby was born to Ruth and Boaz? Ruth 4

8. Who were the twin babies who looked very different? Genesis 25

Free as a Bird

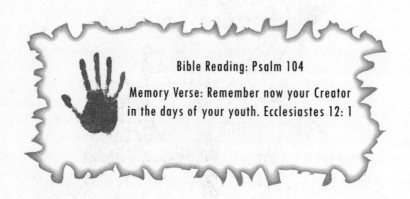

Bible Reading: Psalm 104

Memory Verse: Remember now your Creator in the days of your youth. Ecclesiastes 12: 1

The Jurong Bird Park in Singapore is a wonderful place. Hundreds of visitors go there to see over 8000 birds from Africa, Asia and Europe. The lush tropical vegetation is home to colourful parrots, starlings and bee-eaters.

In a specially cooled section we could view penguins waddling clumsily on land and yet free to swim and dive underwater most gracefully.

The many varieties of parrots and macaws made a magnificent splash of colour in the trees. How wonderful is God's creation. There are more birds and animals than anyone could invent in their minds. Each one is more spectacular and amazing than anything mankind could make. The vibrant colours of the tropical birds,

the graceful elegance of the pink flamingos, the stately power of the black swan - each one an evidence of the might and power of God the Creator.

We were impressed too by the sounds. Such a wonderful variety of songs and noises.

The talking parrots and mynah birds were very amusing when they said things ("Hello" or "Good morning") or gave a very loud wolf whistle!

One centre housed birds of prey – mighty creatures such as golden eagles and hawks – each in individual coops, attached to a short stretch of rope. Most seemed content but one bald-eagle was straining violently at the rope trying to fly free. But the rope kept him firmly trapped.

If only someone had come along and cut the rope, the eagle would have been soaring high.

That bird reminded us of our own plight. We are by nature held firmly under the power of sin and Satan. All our struggles and attempts to be free are not successful. We only gain freedom by the action of someone else – the Lord Jesus Christ. "So if the Son sets you free, you will be free indeed" (John 8: 36).

Christ "cut the rope" which keeps us a slave to sin when he died on the cross. His death broke the power of sin and through him we are set free.

Those who are in Christ are no longer slaves to sin. They have been freed from its dominion and power. "Our soul has escaped as a bird from the snare of the fowlers" (Psalm 124: 7).

REMEMBER TO PRAY

ACTS: Adoration. Confession. Thanks. Supplication.

BIBLE SEARCH

Find the missing words from the chapters. The initials of your answers will spell out the word FREEDOM.

1. Even the sparrow has _____ a home . . . even your altars O Lord of hosts. Psalm 84: 3

2. The _____ brought him bread and meat in the morning, and bread and meat in the evening. 1 Kings 17: 6

3. _____ bird after its kind, every bird of every sort . . . went into the ark. Genesis 7: 14-15

4. Those who wait on the Lord shall renew their strength. They shall mount up with wings like _____. Isaiah 40: 31

5. He saw the spirit of God descending like a _____ and alighting upon him. Matthew 3: 16

5. Are not five sparrows sold for two copper coins? And not _____ of them is forgotten before God. Luke 12: 6

7. In the Lord I put my trust. How can you say to my soul: "Flee as a bird to your _____." Psalm 11: 1

The Broken Foot

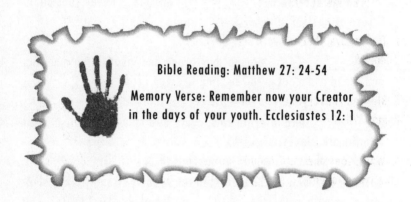

Bible Reading: Matthew 27: 24-54

Memory Verse: Remember now your Creator in the days of your youth. Ecclesiastes 12: 1

Hugh is a farmer on a large farm. He needs to be strong and active to do all his jobs such as looking after sheep, sowing seed and mending machinery.

One day Hugh was working the large machine that shifts grain from the barn into the lorry. Something needed adjusting on the one ton grain bucket at the front, so Hugh nimbly jumped from the cab to do what was necessary. With a sickening thud the massive bucket fell from the machine on to Hugh's foot. What agony he felt. He managed to drag the foot free, pull himself towards the cab and reach for the two-way radio. He gave out the message to the farm office. "I have hurt myself. Can somebody help?"

Hugh was taken to his house, the doctor was called and he was taken quickly to hospital. Just to see him in pain was very upsetting. How much more difficult for him, the one who was suffering. Five bones in his foot had been broken and the healing process would take several months.

When we saw Hugh in pain, we were very affected by it. Just hearing how it happened made us so sad. However, once he got to hospital and was given medicine and treatment, he felt a lot less pain. Now he is much better but we have not forgotten about it.

But have you heard of how Jesus suffered excruciating pain all over his body? He had no sympathetic friends to comfort him; no medicine to relieve the pain, not even a drink of water to satisfy his thirst. The Lord Jesus Christ experienced shameful, painful suffering of the most extreme kind. He suffered willingly because he was obtaining salvation for his people. How does it affect us when we hear about Jesus' suffering? How does it make you feel to hear about Jesus' pain? Do you listen and then forget all about it?

We were so affected by Hugh's sore foot. How much more affected we should be by the pain and misery that Jesus went through for sinners like you and me.

REMEMBER TO PRAY

ACTS: Adoration. Confession. Thanks. Supplication.

BIBLE SEARCH

See if you can find the missing words. The initial letters of your answers will spell out the word SUFFERING.

1. We are heirs . . . if indeed we _____ with him that we may also be glorified together. Romans 8: 17

2. Christ died for the _____. Romans 5: 6

3. He fell on his _____ and prayed saying, "O my Father, if it is possible, let this cup pass from me." Matthew 26: 39

4. Therefore I have set my face like a _____ and I know that I will not be ashamed. Isaiah 50: 7

5. Christ also suffered for us, leaving us an _____. 1 Peter 2: 21

6. The son of man must be delivered into the hands of sinful men, and be crucified and on the third day _____ again. Luke 24: 7

7. Christ, who died . . . also makes _____ for us. Romans 8: 34

8. He prophesied that Jesus would die for the _____. John 11: 51

9. For this purpose I came to this hour. Father, _____ your name. John 12: 27 & 28

114

Meaning of a Cross

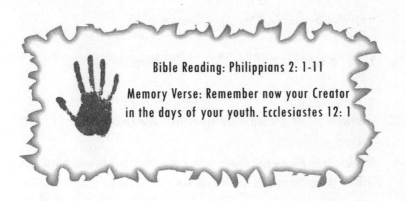

Bible Reading: Philippians 2: 1-11

Memory Verse: Remember now your Creator in the days of your youth. Ecclesiastes 12: 1

When we see a X like this on a piece of paper, it can have several different meanings. When your teacher gives you some arithmetic to do in your work book, she marks it. If you see a X on your page that tells you that you have made a mistake. That cross means, "You are wrong."

If you send your friend a letter or a birthday card you sometimes put a cross after your signature, meaning a kiss. That cross means, "I love you."

People over 18 years of age are allowed to vote for a Member of Parliament in the election. The voting paper lists all the candidates' names. The voter then puts a cross beside the name of the person that he chooses as an MP. That cross means, "I choose this person."

These three meanings of the cross can remind us of different lessons that God is teaching in his word. Paul speaks about another type of cross – the cross of Christ – this is the centre of the gospel message. "May I never boast," he said "except in the cross of our Lord Jesus Christ." It is because of Christ's death on the cross that Paul and every preacher has the message of hope for a sinful world.

The gospel tells us, "You are wrong." We are all sinners. "For all have sinned and fall short of the glory of God" (Romans 3: 23).

But the message does not end there. Throughout the Bible, God sends this message – "I love you." God is love. "This is love, not that we loved God, but that he loved us and sent his Son to be the propitiation for our sins" (1 John 4: 10).

A choice has to be made too. "Choose for yourselves this day whom you will serve . . . but as for me and my house, we will serve the Lord" (Joshua 24: 15).

How good to be like the Psalmist and say, "I have chosen the way of truth" (Psalm 119: 30).

The only way of truth is the Lord Jesus. He said himself, "I am the way, the truth and the life" (John 14: 6). God urges us to "choose life" (Deuteronomy 30: 19). If we make the choice of Jesus we will never be disappointed.

The reason we make the choice of Jesus is that he has first made choice of us – not because of any good thing in us but "according to his good pleasure" (Ephesians 1: 9).

"You did not choose me," said Jesus to his people, "but I chose you" (John 15: 16).

REMEMBER TO PRAY

ACTS: Adoration. Confession. Thanks. Supplication.

BIBLE SEARCH

The message of the cross is central to the gospel. Find the missing words from the following verses. The answers spell out CROSS.

1. God forbid that I should boast except in the cross of our Lord Jesus Christ, by whom the world has been _____ to me and I to the world. Galatians 6: 14

2. That he might _____ them both to God in one body through the cross. Ephesians 2: 16

3. He (Jesus) humbled himself and became _____ to death — even the death of the cross. Philippians 2: 8

4. For the message of the cross is foolishness to those who are perishing, but to us who are being _____ it is the power of God. 1 Corinthians 1: 18

5. Who for the joy that was set before him endured the cross, despising the _____ and has sat down at the right hand of the throne of God. Hebrews 12: 2

The Loving Father

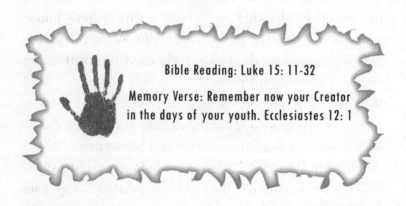

Bible Reading: Luke 15: 11-32

Memory Verse: Remember now your Creator in the days of your youth. Ecclesiastes 12: 1

While we were travelling on a ferry one day we decided to get a breath of fresh air on the top deck. Other passengers had the same idea as us and left their cars to stretch their legs and have a look around. One family had four little children. The father put a little green jacket on a boy of about three years of age and then turned to do the same to the other youngsters. The next thing we noticed was a member of the crew sprinting up the car deck. The little boy had left his father and wandered up the ramp at the front of the boat. Just in time the crew member grabbed him away from danger. How easily he could have toddled into the sea. The crew member returned the boy to his father. Perhaps the father should have scolded the boy for wandering away but he was so glad to see his little boy safe and sound that he just gave him a big hug.

In the Bible we read of a son who ran away. He left home and misused his father's money. When he came to his senses he decided to go back to his father's house and ask to be one of the servants. But instead of giving his son a scolding the father welcomed him with a big hug and a wonderful party. His brother was upset at all the fuss. Why did the father not give his runaway son a row for causing so much heartache and trouble? The father was just so glad to see his son back again.

This is a story that Jesus told to help us to understand how God welcomes us. When we sin we stray away from God but God is so glad to welcome sinners back to himself. Those who repent and seek forgiveness through trusting in the Lord Jesus Christ are more than welcome.

As on-lookers on the ferry, we felt that the little boy should have been told not to do that again. We did not love the boy as his father did. The older brother in the story was displeased at the welcome given to his younger brother. It was wrong of him to feel this way.

We should have the right attitude to other sinners. The offer of mercy is given to them. There is power in the blood of Jesus Christ to cleanse the worst sin.

REMEMBER TO PRAY

ACTS: Adoration. Confession. Thanks. Supplication.

BIBLE SEARCH

The first letters of the missing words spell out a gift from God.

1. We love him because he _____ loved us. 1 John 4: 19

2. For God so loved the world that he gave his _____ begotten Son, that whoever believes in him should not perish but have everlasting life. John 3: 16

3. In his love and in his pity he _____ them. Isaiah 63: 9

4. The life which I now live in the flesh, I live by faith in the Son of God, who loved me and _____ himself for me. Galatians 2: 20

5. May the Lord make you _____ and abound in love. 1 Thessalonians 3: 12

6. I love the Lord because he heard my _____ . Psalm 116: 1

7. He loved them to the _____. John 13: 1

8. Greater love has ____ one than this, than to lay down one's life for his friends. John 15: 13

9. Love does not _____ . 1 Corinthians 13: 4

10. Who shall _____ us from the love of Christ? Romans 8: 35

11. Let us consider one another in order to _____ up love and good works. Hebrews 10: 24

Answer _____

Friends

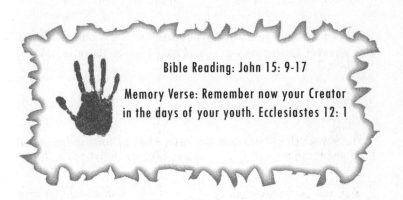

Bible Reading: John 15: 9-17

Memory Verse: Remember now your Creator in the days of your youth. Ecclesiastes 12: 1

Do you have a best friend? Perhaps you play football or go swimming with them. It is great to have a friend to sit beside or to chat to.

A real friend is loyal and kind all the time. They will be your friend when times are hard. When you are in trouble you often find out who your true friends are.

When David was in trouble, he found out what a true friend Jonathan was. King Saul was jealous of David and wanted to kill him. Jonathan, Saul's son, heard about his father's plan and put himself in danger in order to warn David. Because of Jonathan's loyalty David escaped.

We may have many close friends but there is one friend who is the best of all. The Bible tells us that "there is a friend who sticks closer than a brother" (Proverbs 18: 24) and that friend is the Lord Jesus Christ. Our school friends may let us down, but Jesus never will. Jesus has even promised never to leave us!

When Jesus is our friend, he wants us to spend time with him. He wants us to speak to him in prayer and he wants us to listen to him as he speaks to us through his word, the Bible. If Jesus is our friend it will hurt us to hear people say bad words about him. If Jesus is our friend we will want to stand up for him. When Jesus is our friend we will want to tell others how wonderful he is.

Andrew met Jesus one day and realised that he was the Messiah, the one sent by God to be the Saviour. Andrew hurried to find his brother Peter to tell him about Jesus. Jesus was described as "the friend of sinners." We are all sinners but Jesus wants to be our friend. He is so good to us.

If we are the friends of Jesus, he wants us to obey him. "You are my friends if you do whatever I command" (John 15: 14). If we disobey his word and do not believe in him then we cannot call ourselves his friends.

It is lovely to have good ordinary friends but it is more important for us to have Jesus as the friend above all others.

REMEMBER TO PRAY

ACTS: Adoration. Confession. Thanks. Supplication.

BIBLE SEARCH

The first letters of the missing words will spell FRIENDSHIP.

1. Do not _____ your own friend or your father's friend. Proverbs 27: 10

2. He who covers a transgression seeks love, but he who _____ a matter separates friends. Proverbs 17: 9

3. You are my friends ___ you do whatever I command you. John 15: 14

4. Whoever wants to be a friend of the world makes himself an _____ of God. James 4: 4

5. She calls her friends and _____ together saying "Rejoice with me." Luke 15: 9

6. We were well pleased to impart to you not only the gospel of God but also our own lives, because you had become _____ to us. 1 Thessalonians 2: 8

7. No longer do I call you _____ but I have called you friends. John 15: 15

8. Jesus . . . said "Go _____ to your friends and tell them what great things the Lord has done for you." Mark 5: 19

9. May the Lord make you _____ and abound in love to one another and to all. 1 Thessalonians 3: 12

10. Pursue _____ with all people and holiness without which no one will see the Lord. Hebrews 12: 14

Open the Door

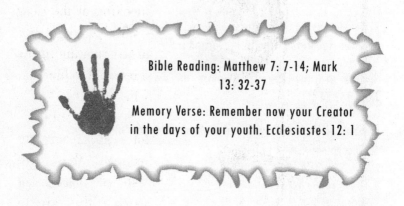

Bible Reading: Matthew 7: 7-14; Mark 13: 32-37

Memory Verse: Remember now your Creator in the days of your youth. Ecclesiastes 12: 1

The other day I went to my friend's door and rang the bell. Nobody came. I tried again – still no reply. I was sure she had said she would be at home. Why was she not answering me? Perhaps she was sleeping or had the radio on very loudly. Or maybe she was just not wanting to be disturbed.

After a while I left and went home. Later I told her what had happened and she told me that her door bell was faulty and had not rung at all.

Jesus speaks about knocking at a door – the door of our heart. "Behold! I stand at the door and knock. If anyone hears my voice and opens the door, I will come in to him and dine with him and he with me" (Revelation 3: 20).

What kind of welcome does Jesus get? Through his word, the Bible, he is knocking at the door – wanting to get our attention, wanting us to respond to him and believe what he says.

Some people do not respond to him because they are "asleep". It's not because they are in bed snoring! Instead this means they are asleep spiritually. They are so comfortable with their sins that they do not pay attention to what God says in his Word, the Bible. We are warned to watch so that when the Son of Man comes he will not find us sleeping (Mark 13: 35-36).

Others are so busy. Their life is full of noise and bustle. They do not hear God speaking to them in his Word. How easy it is to be so interested in other things that we forget to listen to God. "Seek first his kingdom."

Some people hear God's word read or preached and realise that God is speaking to them but refuse to answer. How rude and hurtful. Jesus said to the people of Jerusalem "How often I wanted to gather your children together as a hen gathers her chicks under her wings, but you were not willing" (Matthew 23: 37). The best response to Christ's knocking at the door of our heart is to open the door and say, "Come in."

"If anyone loves me," Jesus said, "he will obey my teaching. My Father will love him, and we will come to him and make our home with him."

REMEMBER TO PRAY

ACTS: Adoration. Confession. Thanks. Supplication.

BIBLE SEARCH

Fill in the gaps. The initial letters spell out the chapter title.

1. Now Peter continued knocking, and when they _____ the door and saw him, they were astonished. Acts 12: 16

2. When the Lord sees the blood on the lintel and on the two door posts, the Lord will _____ over the door. Exodus 12: 23

3. Strive to _____ through the narrow gate. Luke 13: 24

4. Then _____ went with his horses and chariot and he stood at the door of Elisha's house. 2 Kings 5: 9

5. Job said: No sojourner had to lodge in the street, for I have opened my doors to the _____. Job 31: 32

6. I will give her . . . the valley of Achor as a door of _____.
Hosea 2: 15

7. I am the door, if anyone _____ by me, he will be saved.
John 10: 9

8. "You are not also one of this man's _____, are you?"
John 18: 17

9. I have set before you an _____ door and no one can shut.
Revelation 3: 8

10. Knock and it will be _____ to you. Matthew 7: 7

11. As Peter knocked at the door of the gate a girl named _____
came to answer the door. Acts 12: 13

Answer _____   _____   _____

The Armour of God

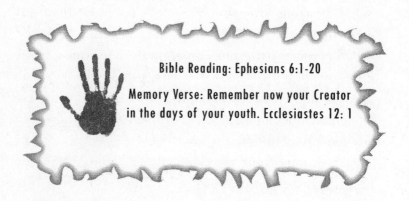

Bible Reading: Ephesians 6:1-20

Memory Verse: Remember now your Creator in the days of your youth. Ecclesiastes 12: 1

There is a very striking location in the north of Scotland called Fort George. It has been an army base for many years and today is the headquarters for one of the Scottish regiments. It is an interesting place to visit.

A room in the museum has the largest collection of Victoria Crosses in the world. The Victoria Cross is the highest honour for bravery that a soldier can be awarded. As well as the medals, stories of how the medals were won are shown on display sheets. Each story tells of dangers and difficulties and of how one man showed bravery in battle. Some medals have been awarded posthumously, that is after the man has died.

The Bible tells us that "greater love has no man than this, that a man lay down his life for his friend." Some of the winners of the Victoria Cross did that but we know of a greater love. The Lord Jesus Christ laid down his life for his enemies. "While we were yet sinners, Christ died for us." He who knew no sin was made sin for us. What amazing love and bravery – far more than any other person.

Other rooms in the museum show the uniforms worn by different soldiers through the ages. Uniform is important for a soldier. He needs to be identified by others and not be confused with the enemy. The uniform has a purpose and has protection for the soldier.

It is important too for the Christian to be identified as that. He should be different from the worldly person. His life should be identified by love, joy, peace, longsuffering, kindness, goodness, faithfulness, gentleness, self-control. Paul speaks of these characteristics as the fruit of the Spirit. If we belong to Jesus Christ, we should be wearing and showing this fruit in our life.

The museum at Fort George has many magnificent swords on display. They were very necessary for a soldier long ago, but are now only used for special celebrations and ceremonies. The Christian too needs what is called in Ephesians the sword of the Spirit which is the Word of God. If we are going to defeat the wickedness of Satan we must attack with the Scriptures. We need to know the Bible to do this and should study God's Word daily. God's Word is "living and powerful, and sharper than any two edged sword, piercing even to the division of soul and spirit, and of the joints and marrow, and is a discerner of the thoughts and intents of the heart" (Hebrews 4: 12).

REMEMBER TO PRAY

ACTS: Adoration. Confession. Thanks. Supplication.

BIBLE SEARCH

Look up Ephesians 6: 10-18. Find out how the Christian soldier is armed to fight against his enemy the devil.

1.   Belt (waisted girded) - _____.

2.   Breastplate - _____.

3.   Shoes - _____   ___   ____

        _____   ___   _____.

4.   Shield - _____.

5.   Helmet - _____.

6.   Sword - _____ — which is the word of God.

Making Your Choice

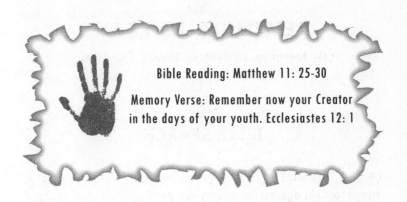

Bible Reading: Matthew 11: 25-30

Memory Verse: Remember now your Creator in the days of your youth. Ecclesiastes 12: 1

You are probably not old enough to vote for a Member of Parliament or a Counsellor but your mum and dad, and everyone over eighteen years of age, is entitled to cast their vote for the person of their choice.

For weeks before an election the candidates will do their best to win votes. They will make promises about what they will do for schools, hospitals, wages or taxes. Many claims are made; many promises are given. Each candidate hopes that the decision will be made to make him or her the new Member of Parliament. The candidate and his agents spend a lot of time and energy in putting forward their case.

The Lord Jesus Christ wants us to make a choice. He wants us to choose him as our Lord and Saviour. This is not a decision that we can make alone but God, the Holy Spirit, works on the heart and the will and enables a sinner to turn from sin and to embrace Jesus Christ who is freely offered in the gospel.

The Lord Jesus makes many claims too. He is the eternal Son of God. Born of the virgin Mary, he lived a perfect sinless life, he was crucified but rose from the dead on the third day and was seen by many people before he ascended up into heaven. Even now he prays and intercedes for his people.

All Jesus' claims are true. There are no exaggerations. He doesn't tell untrue stories to make him look better than he is. Jesus is perfect. He is the best – that's true.

Jesus gives many promises too. "I will never leave you or forsake you." "My peace I give you." "My God will meet all your needs according to his glorious riches in Christ Jesus." "Believe in the Lord Jesus Christ and you will be saved."

The Bible is full of precious promises made to believers, i.e. people who have made the right choice of believing in Christ.

The Lord Jesus does not make a promise that he cannot keep. Many of the election candidates will disappoint us – even the ones who win on the day. They make mistakes: they may be unable to do what they intended; they may even have lied about what they said they would do in order to win the vote. The Lord Jesus will never disappoint those who follow him. He is wise, powerful, holy, just, good and true in all he does and says. Give him your vote.

REMEMBER TO PRAY

ACTS: Adoration. Confession. Thanks. Supplication.

BIBLE SEARCH

Fill in the missing words. The first letters will spell out another word — PROMISES.

1. Be anxious for nothing, but in everything, by prayer and supplication, with thanksgiving, let your requests be made known to God. And the _____ of God, which surpasses all understanding, will guard your hearts and minds through Christ Jesus. Philippians 4: 6-7

2. Come to me, all you who labour and are heavy laden, and I will give you _____. Matthew 11: 28

3. Give me understanding and I shall keep your law; indeed I shall _____ it with my whole heart. Psalm 119: 34

4. Many sorrows shall be to the wicked, but he who trusts in the Lord _____ shall surround him. Psalm 32: 10

5. May the Lord make you _____ and abound in love to one another. 1 Thessalonians 3: 12

6. Be not dismayed, for I am your God. I will _____ you, yes I will help you. Isaiah 41: 10

8. For the Lord your God is he who goes with you to fight for you against your _____ to save you. Deuteronomy 20: 4

9. Cast your burden on the Lord and he shall _____ you. Psalm 55: 22

Meal with Friends

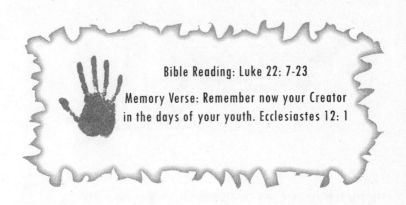

Bible Reading: Luke 22: 7-23

Memory Verse: Remember now your Creator in the days of your youth. Ecclesiastes 12: 1

What a treat it is to be invited out for a meal with friends. We enjoy different food and it is especially good for mums to have a rest from the cooking. It is just as enjoyable to have friends come to our house for a meal. It is good fun getting ready, preparing something special to eat and making sure that everything looks nice.

Having a meal together is a real sign of friendship between the host and the guest.

The friendship between God and his people is described in a similar way. "Behold! I stand at the door and knock," says the Lord, "if anyone hears my voice and opens the door, I will come in and eat with him and he with me."

The relationship between God and his church is depicted by the act of eating supper together.

When friends eat together it is not just the food that is important. It is a great opportunity to speak together – to give news, to share problems, to encourage one another.

Jesus ate meals in the home of his friends Mary, Martha and Lazarus. One time Martha got harassed in preparing the food while her sister sat and listened to Jesus' conversation. Jesus told Martha that Mary had chosen what is better.

Jesus ate supper with his disciples on the night of his betrayal. The special Passover feast, when the Jewish people remembered their deliverance from Egypt in the time of Moses, was prepared by Peter and John in an upper room in Jerusalem.

At this last supper with his friends, Jesus started what we call the Lord's Supper. The bread is to remind us of Jesus Christ's body, broken for his people. The wine represents Jesus Christ's blood, shed for his people. In churches all over the world this meal of bread and wine is celebrated. It nourishes and strengthens the Lord's people. Those who love the Lord sit at his table as his guests. He has commanded them to do so. "Do this in remembrance of me."

After Jesus rose from the dead, his disciples saw him on several occasions. One day some of them were out on the Sea of Tiberias fishing, but with no success. They saw a man on the shore who called out to them to throw the net out again on the right side of the ship. When they did so they caught a huge number of fish. John then realised that the man on the shore was the Lord Jesus. Jesus had prepared breakfast there on the shore. Fish was already cooking on a fire of coals but Jesus asked them to bring some of their fish too. The risen Lord served them breakfast of bread and fish.

What a lovely way to show the disciples his friendship. We should remember that he tells us "As I have loved you so you must love one another."

Look out for an opportunity today to show love in a practical way to a friend.

REMEMBER TO PRAY

ACTS: Adoration. Confession. Thanks. Supplication.

BIBLE SEARCH

1. What food did Jesus use to feed 5,000 people in a desert place? Matthew 14: 17

2. In Jesus' parable what was served by the king at his son's wedding feast? Matthew 22: 4

3. When the prodigal son came home, what was prepared for the celebration feast? Luke 15: 23

4. Jesus performed his first miracle at a marriage feast. What did he do? John 2: 9

5. Abraham had an unexpected visit from three men who brought him a message from God. What meal did he give them? Genesis 18: 6-8

6. What favourite meal did Isaac ask Esau to prepare for him? Genesis 27: 3-4

7. What did Rebekah make for Jacob to give to his father Isaac? Genesis 27: 9

8. When Joseph entertained his brothers to a meal in the palace in Egypt, which brother was given five times as much as the others? Genesis 43: 34

Rabbits

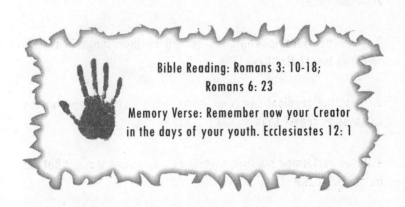

Bible Reading: Romans 3: 10-18;
Romans 6: 23

Memory Verse: Remember now your Creator
in the days of your youth. Ecclesiastes 12: 1

Have you ever noticed any rabbits running around the countryside? Near our home we often see these little animals at the roadside bobbing through the hedges. They look so loveable, so soft and furry – I just feel like taking one home with me for a pet.

My husband is a farmer and he thinks differently about rabbits. He does not like them at all. If they get into his field of carrots they do a lot of damage. Time, money and effort is spent in growing the field of carrots for the supermarkets so a special fence is erected round the field. A rabbit would be able to burrow underneath so the fence is dug 18 inches underground. Some rabbits still find their way through the fence so in the early

morning a man goes out with a gun to shoot them. It is the only way to protect the field of carrots. What drastic action!

Sin is a bit like the rabbits. There are so many of them and if we do nothing about it they become more and more numerous. Sin can seem so pleasant and nice to us. We can enjoy it and perhaps see no harm in it at all.

It can seem better to us to have our own way rather than obey our mum and dad. We might enjoy taking someone else's toy or packet of sweets, but that is sin and sin is harmful to us.

We have a duty to take action against sin – to do all we can to ensure that it does not get into our lives and spoil our souls. Nothing we do though can go far enough to destroy sin. The only one who can do that is the Lord Jesus Christ. He took the drastic action on our behalf when he laid down his life on the cross at Calvary. He took the punishment of sin. What he did will cleanse us from the guilt and power of sin. "He who covers his sins will not prosper; but whoever confesses and forsakes them will have mercy" (Proverbs 28: 13).

Sin is very serious. It can result in lots of damage to our lives, but God has shown mercy to his people through Jesus Christ. "The wages of sin is death but the gift of God is eternal life in Christ Jesus our Lord" (Romans 6: 23).

The little bunnies look so harmless yet they do lots of harm. Many of our sins look harmless too but remember they do a lot of damage. Take the advice of God's Word and flee from all sin to the Lord Jesus Christ who alone can deal with this big problem for us.

REMEMBER TO PRAY

ACTS: Adoration. Confession. Thanks. Supplication.

BIBLE SEARCH

The initial letters of the answers spell out SIN and FORGIVE.

1. Moses . . . chose rather to _____ affliction with the people of God than to enjoy the passing pleasures of sin. Hebrews 11: 25

2. Hide your face from my sins and blot out all my _____. Psalm 51: 9

3. How shall we escape if we _____ so great a salvation. Hebrews 2: 3

4. For whoever finds me finds life and obtains _____ from the Lord. Proverbs 8: 35

5. I am too ashamed . . . for ___ iniquities have risen higher than our heads. Ezra 9: 6

6. Do not let sin _____ in your mortal body. Romans 6: 12

7. For all have sinned and fall short of the _____ of God. Romans 3: 23

8. Pardon my _____ for it is great. Psalm 25: 11

9. The _____ of the Lord is powerful. Psalm 29: 4

10. For the wages of sin is death, but the gift of God is _____ life in Christ Jesus our Lord. Romans 6: 23

Cities of Refuge

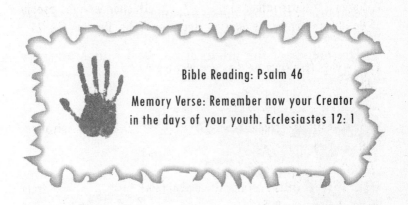

Bible Reading: Psalm 46

Memory Verse: Remember now your Creator in the days of your youth. Ecclesiastes 12: 1

In a little back street in the town of Ripon in Yorkshire there is a very interesting stone monument. It is all that remains of a stone cross known as the Sharow Cross. In centuries gone by the Church of St. Wilfrid (now known as Ripon Cathedral) was a sanctuary for fugitives. Anyone within one mile of this church was safe from his pursuers. Stone crosses were placed all round the church at a distance of one mile – within this boundary was the place of refuge. The Sharow Cross is the only one that is still in existence in Ripon.

The provision of a place of refuge like this goes back to Bible times. In Numbers chapter 35 we read about the cities of refuge that God provided for people who had killed someone accidentally. If a man managed to find his way to one of these six cities, then he would be safe from the relative seeking revenge.

The Lord Jesus is a refuge for all who trust him. We are all guilty of sin and if we are outside of Christ we are in great danger. But if we take advantage of the safety only to be found in Jesus then we are safe for all eternity.

The names of the different cities of refuge are very interesting.

Kadesh means "consecrated" or "holy". Our refuge, the Lord Jesus, is the truly holy One.

Shechem means "a shoulder". This reminds us of power. The prophet Isaiah, when he speaks about Jesus Christ, told us that "the government will be on his shoulder". He has all power.

Kirjath-arba or *Hebron* signifies fellowship. Jesus is the best person to be friends with as he is the one who really knows and loves us.

Bezer is a fort or a strong place. The Lord is a refuge and strength to all who trust in him.

Ramoth stands for "high" or "exalted". There is no name higher or better than that of the Lord Jesus. At the name of Jesus every knee shall bow.

Golan means "joy". The Lord Jesus is the joy and rejoicing of the Christian's heart.

So the names of each of the cities of refuge remind us in some way of Jesus, the Saviour of his people – the only safe refuge.

REMEMBER TO PRAY

ACTS: Adoration. Confession. Thanks. Supplication.

BIBLE SEARCH

Find the missing words. The initial letters of the answers spell out the word REFUGE.

1. The Lord has been my defence and my God the _____ of my refuge. Psalm 94: 22

2. The _____ God is your refuge. Deuteronomy 33:27

3. O Lord, my strength and my _____ my refuge in the day of affliction. Jeremiah 16: 19

4. God is your refuge and _____ are the everlasting arms. Deuteronomy 33: 27

5. _____ is our refuge and strength, a very present help in trouble. Psalm 46: 1

6. How shall we _____ if we neglect so great a salvation? Hebrews 2: 3

On the Doorstop

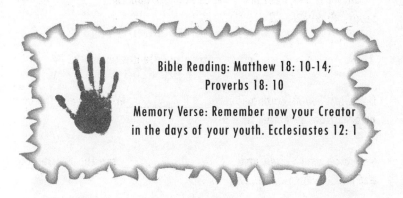

Bible Reading: Matthew 18: 10-14;
Proverbs 18: 10

Memory Verse: Remember now your Creator
in the days of your youth. Ecclesiastes 12: 1

Angus is an old shepherd (over ninety years old now), living in the north west of Scotland. At lambing time Angus would spend many hours, out in all weathers, helping the ewes and making sure that the new lambs had shelter.

Last April at lambing time, Angus had a very bad dose of flu. He had to stay indoors. He could not go out to help his sheep as usual. Late one evening Angus looked out of the window and noticed that one ewe had just lambed. It was stormy and dark. Angus was anxious about the lamb but he was too weak to go out to look after it.

"That lamb will be dead by morning," he thought sadly. Angus had to go back to bed but early next morning when he got up, he looked out of the window. There was no sign of that lamb or the mother. What could have happened? Angus opened the door and there on the step was the lamb being sheltered by its mother – comfortable and safe. The sheep knew the shepherd well, knew that he would care for her and her young lamb. She made her way to the place of safety, the shepherd's door.

Jesus is the good shepherd for his sheep, those who trust in him. We will be safe when we keep as close to him as we can. We should know how kind and good he is to us and should want to be as close to him as possible. "Come to me, all you who are weary and burdened," he says, "and I will give you rest."

Troubles can make life difficult for us. We must come to Jesus and he will help us. Our sinful hearts, actions and words can lead us into difficulties. We must come to

Jesus with them too. Only he can wash away our sin and make us fit to meet God.

Samuel Rutherford, a preacher in Scotland many years ago, once said, "I will go to the door of Christ and if I perish there, I will perish where no man ever perished before." That was how he expressed his confidence in Jesus the Saviour. We can make our way to the 'doorstep' of Jesus. We can find safety in him. How do we do that? We can do that by reading his Word, the Bible, and thinking about it. We can do it by praying to him at any time, asking for forgiveness, thanking him for his kindness, casting all our care upon him for he cares for us.

The good shepherd, the Lord Jesus, is never tired. He is always ready to help us when we need him.

REMEMBER TO PRAY

ACTS: Adoration. Confession. Thanks. Supplication.

BIBLE SEARCH

Find the missing words from the texts. Hint — all the answers begin with the same letter.

1. He will feed his flock like a shepherd: He will gather the _____ with his arm. Isaiah 40: 11

2. He makes me to ____ down in green pastures. He _____ me beside the still waters. Psalm 23: 2

3. I am the good shepherd. The good shepherd gives his _____ for the sheep. John 10: 11

4. By this we know _____, because he _____ down his _____ for us. 1 John 3: 16

5. I have gone astray like a _____ sheep. Seek your servant. Psalm 119: 176

6. The _____ is my shepherd; I shall not want. Psalm 23: 1

The Sundial

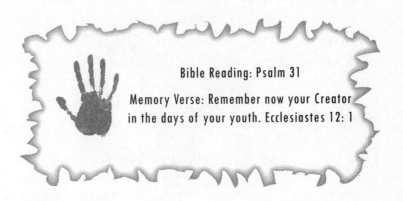

Bible Reading: Psalm 31

Memory Verse: Remember now your Creator in the days of your youth. Ecclesiastes 12: 1

We had a special anniversary recently and were given a beautiful sundial as a present. It is made from red sandstone with the device on top made from bronze. This can be used to tell the time during the hours of sunlight. The fixed metal arm casts a shadow on the dial which is marked out in hours. Provided the sundial has been fixed properly, with the arm pointing from north to south then this can tell the time fairly accurately according to the position of the sun.

Our sundial also has the words *TEMPUS FUGIT* cast in the metal. These Latin words mean "time flies". This is a reminder for anyone looking at the sundial that the time of our life passes very quickly. Older people often

complain about how quickly time passes whereas you perhaps feel that the time is just crawling very slowly until your birthday or holiday. When we feel that time is passing quickly it should make us realise how precious each moment is. Ethan, the writer of Psalm 89, prays to the Lord to show himself to him, remembering how short his time is. We too should pray to God to bless us and use us in his service, because our time is short.

Paul warns us in Ephesians to be careful how we behave from day to day, using each day wisely. "Redeeming the time, because the days are evil." We have a responsibility to use each hour that God gives us, in a way that is pleasing to him. Time is a gift from God and should be used for him. Think about how you can spend your time doing things for God.

We look at the clock many times a day to find out if it is time to leave for school or have our meal. "Is it time yet?" we ask. Sometimes the answer is "No, it is not time yet." But if our question was "Is it time to seek the Lord?" the answer would always be "YES". The Bible says "NOW is the time of God's favour, NOW is the day of salvation."

The words on the sundial *Tempus Fugit* should remind us of more than just the quick passing of time. It should warn us to use the time we have for the most important thing in life – the salvation of our soul. This is found only by trusting in the Lord Jesus Christ and loving him for what he has done on the cross for sinners like us.

REMEMBER TO PRAY

ACTS: Adoration. Confession. Thanks. Supplication.

BIBLE SEARCH

In the Bible times, the hours were counted from daybreak to sunset. The 3rd hour would be equivalent to 9 a.m., the 6th hour to midday . Find the times at which the following events took place.

1. When Andrew met Jesus he went to see where he lived. He decided to stay because it was late. What time was it? John 1: 29

2. At what time did Jesus sit on Jacob's well to rest and speak to the woman of Samaria? John 4: 6

3. At what hour did the nobleman's son begin to get better? John 4: 52

4. At what hour of the day was Jesus crucified? Mark 15: 25

5. At what hour on the same day did darkness fall over the land? Mark 15: 33

6. At what hour did Jesus die? Mark 15: 34

7. When did Peter begin to preach his sermon on the Day of Pentecost? Acts 2: 15

8. What time was known as the hour of prayer? Acts 3: 1

9. At what time did Peter see a vision which encouraged him to share the gospel with Cornelius the centurion? Acts 10: 9

10. At what hour of the night did the soldiers take Paul to Felix the governor? Acts 23 :23

Engraving that Lasts

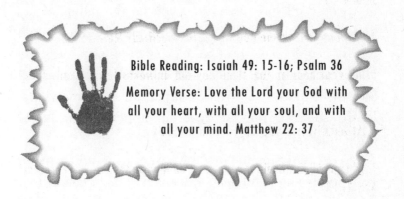

Bible Reading: Isaiah 49: 15-16; Psalm 36

Memory Verse: Love the Lord your God with all your heart, with all your soul, and with all your mind. Matthew 22: 37

I have an old watch in my jewellery box. It no longer works but it has engraved on the back the words "From Duncan December 1917". It was a gift that my mother received from her brother who was then a soldier in the First World War. The watch is of little value but because of the engraving I like to keep it.

If your school team wins the inter-school sports the name of the school and the date would be engraved on the winning silver cup.

Metal is engraved with initials, dates or names to commemorate or remember an important occasion like a wedding or winning a competition. It is a way of making sure that we do not forget the important occasion.

Sometimes if I need to remember to phone someone or buy something in the shop I will write it on my hand with a ballpoint pen. That washes off later of course. God tells us in the book of Isaiah that he will never forget his people. "I have inscribed you on the palms of my hands" (Isaiah 49: 16). The Lord has done so much for his people. The most wonderful thing of all was the Lord Jesus dying on the cross to take the punishment for the sins of those who trust in him. After three days the Lord Jesus rose from the dead and appeared on several occasions to his disciples.

On one occasion the disciples were in an upper room. They felt frightened because Jesus had just been killed. Everything had gone wrong . . . or so they thought. Just then Jesus appeared! He was alive.

"Peace be with you," he said to them. Then he showed them his hands and his side. His hands were deeply marked, showing the scars of the nails which had been driven through his hands and nailed him to the cross.

How deeply these hands had been marked. Jesus has engraved us onto his hands because his hands were nailed to the cross and he loves us with a love that will never end.

The engraving on a wedding ring tells of the love a bridegroom has for his bride. But that engraving might wear away over the years and become impossible to read.

The marks on the hands of Jesus Christ tell of an even greater love that the Saviour has for all his people when he gave his life as a ransom for many.

REMEMBER TO PRAY

ACTS: Adoration. Confession. Thanks. Supplication.

BIBLE SEARCH

The initial letters spell out something that Jesus will never do with his people.

1. Unless I see in his hands the print of the nails and put my _____ into the print of the nails, and put my hand into his side, I will not believe it. John 20: 25

2. You shall take two _____ stones and engrave on them the names of the sons of Israel. Exodus 28: 9

3. I have been young and now I am old, yet I have not seen the _____ forsaken nor his descendents begging bread. Psalm 37: 25

4. The tablets were the work of God, the writing was the writing of ____, engraved on the tablets. Exodus 32: 16

5. On the opening were _____ but the panels were square, not round. 1 Kings 7: 31

6. The sin of Judah is written with a pen of iron, with the point of a diamond it is engraved on the _____ of their heart. Jeremiah 17: 1

Answer _____

Missed Out

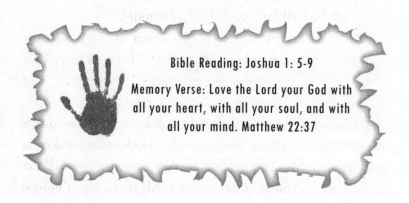

Bible Reading: Joshua 1: 5-9

Memory Verse: Love the Lord your God with all your heart, with all your soul, and with all your mind. Matthew 22:37

Our daughter, Wilma, was awarded a Bronze medal under the Duke of Edinburgh's Award Scheme. She worked at the local hospital, learnt to look after pigs, improved her badminton playing and went on an expedition in the mountains, camping out overnight.

The Mayor of the town was to present the awards to about fifty young people so there was quite a bit of excitement. All the youngsters were looking forward to receiving their certificates and badges.

Name after name was called out. One by one the girl or boy went up to the stage and everyone clapped. Wilma sat patiently in her seat, waiting for her name to be called. Eventually the announcer said, "And lastly James Macdonald from Highland Outdoor Centre."

Wilma's name had not been called yet. What had happened? What a disappointment!

Speeches were made and a vote of thanks was given. Everything was finished as all the people went to the back of the hall for tea and refreshments.

We went to the man who had read out the names to ask if Wilma's name had been on the list. "I am so sorry," he said, "I forgot to turn over the page." Two names had been omitted. The man had made a mistake.

How easy it is to make a mistake – to miss out a name or to forget to turn a page. God never makes a mistake. At the Day of Judgement every name will be called out. No one will be omitted. All will appear before the judgement seat of God. To some he will say, "Depart from me you cursed into the everlasting fire prepared for the devil and his angels" (Matthew 25: 41).

But to those who love and trust him he will say, "Come you who are blessed by my Father, inherit the kingdom prepared for you from the foundation of the world" (Matthew 25: 34). No one who belongs to Jesus will be disappointed at the last day. Jesus said to his Father, "Those whom you have given me I have kept, and none of them is lost." His people are never forgotten. "I have engraved you on the palms of my hands," he said.

Wilma's story has a happy ending. Her father was concerned about the situation and spoke to the Provost at the end. "I did enjoy giving all these boys and girls their awards," he said. "Well," said Wilma's Dad, "there are two young people here who were missed out."

"That will never do," said the Provost.

"We will reconvene the meeting and give them the awards right away."

So with a great many apologies, Wilma and her schoolfriend were presented with their awards after all.

REMEMBER TO PRAY

ACTS: Adoration. Confession. Thanks. Supplication.

BIBLE SEARCH

Find the missing words. Clue — the answers spell the word AWARD.

1. Do not be afraid _____. I am your shield, your exceeding great reward. Genesis 15: 1

2. The labourer is _____ of his wages. 1 Timothy 5: 18

3. Do you not know that those who run in a race ____ run, but one receives the prize? 1 Corinthians 9: 24

4. The Lord _____ your work and a full reward be given you by the Lord the God of Israel, under whose wings you have come for refuge. Ruth 2: 12

5. Rejoice in that ____ and leap for joy! For indeed your reward is great in heaven. Luke 6: 23

The Orchestra

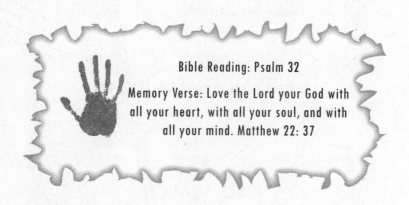

Bible Reading: Psalm 32

Memory Verse: Love the Lord your God with all your heart, with all your soul, and with all your mind. Matthew 22: 37

Have you ever heard a full orchestra playing? All the instruments are made of different materials and make a variety of noises. Yet under a talented conductor the orchestra can make a sound which is beautiful and complete.

Each musician has a different part to play. If the violinists do not bother to play, the piece does not sound so good. If the trombonist plays a wrong note, everyone notices. Every instrument is important – even the tiny triangle has its part to play to make the whole orchestra sound the way that the composer planned.

God has composed a plan for his people. Each Christian has a part to play in spreading the good news of Jesus Christ. Some people feel that they have a very

small part but each small part is vital to the complete symphony of God's plan.

The conductor knows the music well and leads the musicians to play their part. God leads and guides each believer in his life. "I will instruct you and teach you in the way that you should go," he tells the Christian.

It is important for the players to keep their eye on the conductor while they are playing so that they keep the timing right. It is important for the Christian to keep his eyes firmly fixed on Jesus – looking unto Jesus the author and finisher of his faith – so that he does not stray away from what God wants him to do.

An orchestra playing a beautiful piece of music brings great pleasure to those who listen. Jesus tells us that there is joy in heaven when one sinner repents and turns to God. If each Christian does his part with God's help to spread the gospel, this will be pleasing to God.

REMEMBER TO PRAY

ACTS: Adoration. Confession. Thanks. Supplication.

BIBLE SEARCH

Several musical instruments are mentioned in the Bible. Can you find some of them?

1. What did David play? 1 Samuel 16: 23

2. What instrument made a certain sound to prepare soldiers for battle? 1 Corinthians 14: 8

3. What did Miriam and the Israelite women play? Exodus 15: 20

4. What did Asaph make a sound with before the ark of the covenant of God? 1 Chronicles 16: 5

5. Which two instruments were used when Solomon was anointed as king? 1 Kings 1: 39-40

6. Nebuchadnezzar commanded the people to bow down to the image of gold when they heard which musical instruments? Daniel 3: 5

Safely Home

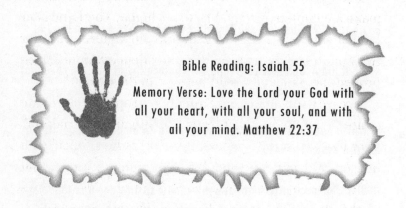

Bible Reading: Isaiah 55

Memory Verse: Love the Lord your God with all your heart, with all your soul, and with all your mind. Matthew 22:37

Peter was a bomber pilot flying a Lancaster plane during the Second World War. He made many journeys over enemy country. One time after a raid, the navigator gave him directions for home but after a short time, Peter was anxious about their progress.

"Check that we are going in the right direction," he instructed the navigator.

"Yes, we are on the right course," was the reply. Ten minutes later Peter was even more unsure.

"Double check our direction," he ordered.

"Heading straight for England," was the reply.

Peter's next command was to the radio operator.

"Break radio silence," he said. "Get a beam to home and check our direction."

The radio operator came back with the startling news. "We will have to make a 180 degree turn. We are on the right line but going in the wrong direction."

Peter had been right to be worried. The plane had to make a complete turn and head for home. The Lancaster landed safely in England with only enough fuel left for two minutes of flying time. If radio silence had not been broken the outcome would have been disastrous.

Are we going in the right direction in our journey of life or are we on the way that leads to death and destruction? How will we know? We have to break 'radio silence' with heaven and pray to God. We must contact him to put us in the right direction. If we are out of touch then we are heading in the wrong direction. His message to us is clear. "Seek the Lord while he may be found, call on him while he is near" (Isaiah 55: 6). "Turn, turn from your evil ways! Why will you die?" (Ezekiel 33:11).

If our lives are heading in the wrong direction then we are living dangerously and foolishly. If we are going in the right direction then we are living hopefully and waiting for a better life with the Lord. This we can do by looking to Jesus, the author and finisher of our faith.

If we make contact while mercy is to be found, then we can be sure of a safe homecoming to heaven at last.

REMEMBER TO PRAY

ACTS: Adoration. Confession. Thanks. Supplication.

BIBLE SEARCH

Who were the people who 'broke radio silence' with heaven and made the following prayers to God?

1. Lord, remember me when you come into your kingdom. Luke 23: 42

2. God be merciful to me, a sinner. Luke 18: 13

3. Oh, that you would bless me indeed and enlarge my territory! That your hand would be with me and that you would keep me from evil that I may not cause pain. 1 Chronicles 4: 10

4. Therefore you are great O Lord God. For there is none like you. 2 Samuel 7: 22

5. Hear me, O Lord, hear me, that this people may know that you are the Lord God. 1 Kings 18: 37

6. My heart rejoices in the Lord; my horn is exalted in the Lord. 1 Samuel 2: 1

7. May the good Lord provide atonement for everyone who prepares his heart to seek God. 2 Chronicles 30: 18-19

8. Lord, save me. Matthew 14: 30

Pottery

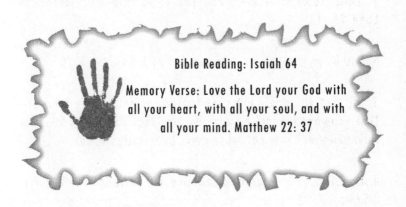

Bible Reading: Isaiah 64

Memory Verse: Love the Lord your God with all your heart, with all your soul, and with all your mind. Matthew 22: 37

Have you ever watched a skilled potter working at a wheel? They can turn a shapeless lump of clay into a jug, a bowl or a vase.

I recently visited a local pottery where the whole process could be watched. The potter took a piece of dull clay – quite ugly really – moistened it and threw it on to the spinning potter's wheel. He then worked at it patiently, pulling and shaping and cutting bits out. Eventually a finished vase was removed from the wheel.

It was then left to dry and fired in a kiln to harden and strengthen it. After glazing and more firing, the vase would be ready for use. In the skilful hands of the potter, an ugly lump of clay had been turned into a beautiful and useful piece of pottery.

The prophet Isaiah uses the picture of the potter to teach us a lesson. God is the potter and we are the clay. God can take the rough, ugly raw material of our lives and make something from it that is useful and beautiful. He is our Creator. He is the one who also gives us new life, and this new life is to give service and glory to our Creator and Redeemer.

The potter can decide what he is to make with the lump of clay. He could make an ornamental vase, a sugar bowl or a vinegar jar, each with a different appearance and use. God has control over his creatures. He placed us in different situations and has given us different work to do. We should not ask God, "Why have you made me like this?" Paul says in the letter to the Romans "Does not the potter have power over the clay?" In the same way God has power over his creation.

The firing of the clay in the kiln is vitally important for making the pot strong.

The fire of testing and trouble make the Christian stronger. Paul could say that he actually gloried in troubles because they produced patience, then experience and then hope, which does not make us ashamed. This fire is not to harm Christians but to make them more useful for the Lord's service.

REMEMBER TO PRAY

ACTS: Adoration. Confession. Thanks. Supplication.

BIBLE SEARCH

We can use pottery for many different purposes e.g. to hold sugar, or salt or flowers. Pots were used in Bible times for different purposes too. Find out some of the uses for the items made by a potter.

1. What did the woman of Samaria carry in her jar? John 4: 28

2. What did Moses tell Aaron to put in a jar, to place before the Lord? Exodus 16: 33

3. What did Gideon bring in a pot to present to the Lord? Judges 6: 19

4. What was in the pot that the widow told Elisha was the only thing she had left in the house? 2 Kings 4: 2

5. God has great power. He makes the sea like a pot of what? Job 41: 31

6. What was in the bowls and cups offered to the Rechabites, which they refused? Jeremiah 35: 5

The Most Amazing Thing

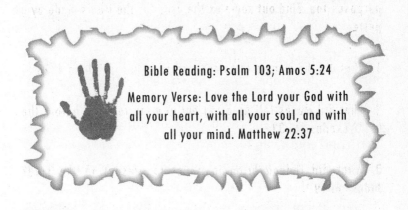

Bible Reading: Psalm 103; Amos 5:24

Memory Verse: Love the Lord your God with all your heart, with all your soul, and with all your mind. Matthew 22:37

Recently we went to visit an old friend who had been a missionary for many years in Zimbabwe. She told us the story of Mzabo, an African Christian lady, she had known well.

One day Mzabo had to travel to Durban. She had never left her village before and it was a long and tiring journey through many towns and cities. When she came back home she was asked, "What was the most amazing thing you saw?" Would it be the huge buildings, the motor cars or the train engine?

Mzabo replied, "The most amazing thing I saw was the sea. It stretched as far as I could see yet always came towards me. It reminded me of the mercies of God – vast and immeasurable yet always coming towards me."

What a lovely thought and what an encouragement for that old African lady on her difficult journey. What an encouraging thought for us too.

God's compassion and pity for those who are guilty is great. "To the Lord our God belong mercy and forgiveness, though we have rebelled against him" (Daniel 9: 9). "As far as the east is from the west, so far has he removed our transgressions from us" (Psalm 103: 12). The distance between east and west is immeasurable – no matter how far east you go you can still go further east. North and south can be measured. But not east and west. Neither can you measure God's love and mercy – it is immeasurable.

Look at the ocean – the waves never stop. "Let your tender mercies come to me," said David to the Lord, "that I may live."

Jeremiah too was conscious of God's mercies for every breath. "It is of the Lord's mercies that we are not consumed," he said, "because his compassions fail not."

Next time you go to the seaside remember the great mercies of God. When you feel the waves lapping over your feet remember how God sends his great mercy right to where you are, through his dear Son the Lord Jesus.

REMEMBER TO PRAY

ACTS: Adoration. Confession. Thanks. Supplication.

BIBLE SEARCH

The mercies of God are spoken about a great deal in the Bible. Find out for yourself some of what is told us by looking up the following verses. The missing words spell out MERCIES.

1. Yet in your _____ mercies you did not forsake them in the wilderness. Nehemiah 9: 19

2. Through the Lord's mercies we are not consumed . . . they are new _____ morning. Lamentations 3: 22-23

3. _____ , O Lord, your tender mercies and your lovingkindnesses. Psalm 25: 6

4. Blessed be the God and Father of our Lord Jesus Christ, the Father of mercies and the God of all _____. 2 Corinthians 1: 3

5. Bless the Lord, O my soul . . . who forgives all your _____ , . . . who crowns you with lovingkindness and tender mercies. Psalm 103: 2-4

6. I have inclined my heart to perform your statutes forever, to the very ____. Psalm 119:112

7. I will _____ of the mercies of the Lord for ever. Psalm 89: 1

Three Gardens

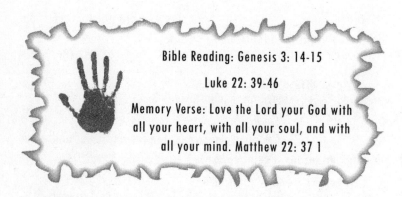

Bible Reading: Genesis 3: 14-15

Luke 22: 39-46

Memory Verse: Love the Lord your God with all your heart, with all your soul, and with all your mind. Matthew 22: 37 1

We have had visitors from Australia staying with us recently and have been showing them some of the beautiful places near our home. One lovely trip was to Inverewe Gardens on the west coast of Scotland. These gardens are quite far north and in a part of the country that is mountainous and rocky. What a surprise to see palms trees, bamboo shoots and exotic ferns as well as the rhododendrons, azaleas and numerous other colourful and interesting plants.

Foresight and hard work on the part of the founder of the garden and many other people and the climatic effect of the warm Gulf stream on that part of the west coast, make this garden especially attractive and unusual. Many visitors come from all over the world to see the gardens at Inverewe. People get great enjoyment from walking among the plants, admiring them, smelling the perfume, touching the bark on the trees and hearing the waterfalls and birds.

When God created Adam and Eve, he planted a wonderful garden for them to enjoy, the Garden of Eden. There were beautiful trees, good to look at and good for food. A river flowed through it to give the plants enough water. Adam was given the pleasant work of looking after the garden.

In this garden God had fellowship with Adam and Eve, created in his image. They were free to eat of all the fruit of the garden except the tree of the knowledge of good and evil. Adam and Eve sinned by disobeying God's command. This resulted in their separation from God and their being put out of this wonderful garden. Cherubim and a flaming sword guarded the way to the tree of life. Adam and Eve were banished. Sin had entered the world – sin which God hates.

Sin must be punished. One of the punishments was the cursing of the ground. Tending a garden now means hard work. Thorns and weeds and thistles cause problems but God is still merciful in giving food from the ground – fruit, vegetables and crops. God pronounced a curse on Satan, who in the form of a serpent, tempted Adam and Eve to sin. "I will put enmity between you and the woman, and between your seed and her seed; he shall bruise your head, and you shall bruise his heel" (Genesis 3: 15). In the middle of this curse is a message of hope. The woman's seed is Christ. He would one day defeat Satan with a fatal blow to the head but would suffer much pain himself in doing that.

Some of Christ's suffering occurred in another garden, the Garden of Gethsemane, where many olive trees grew. For many hours Jesus was in deep distress and sorrow as he faced up to the coming anger of God against sin. This made Jesus' soul very troubled and anxious but Jesus didn't give up. Jesus took the punishment for his people's sin. He died for the ungodly. Part of the gospel promise made in the Garden of Eden was fulfilled as Christ suffered in the Garden of Gethsemane, on his way to Calvary where he fully defeated Satan.

REMEMBER TO PRAY

ACTS: Adoration. Confession. Thanks. Supplication.

BIBLE SEARCH

Look up the following verses to find things that we might find in a garden today.

1. The desert shall rejoice and blossom as the _____. Isaiah 35: 1

2. If then God so clothes the _____ which today is in the field, and tomorrow is thrown into the oven; how much more will he clothe you, O you of little faith. Luke 12: 28

3. The daughter of Zion is left as a booth in a vineyard, as a hut in a garden of _____ , as a besieged city. Isaiah 1: 8

4. Your word is a lamp to my feet and a light to my _____. Psalm 119: 105

5. Consider the _____ of the field, how they grow, they neither toil nor spin. Matthew 6: 28

6. I made myself gardens and orchards, and I planted all kinds of _____ _____ in them. Ecclesiastes 2: 5

7. As for man, his days are like grass: as a _____ of the field, so he flourishes. Psalm 103: 15

7. Ahab spoke unto Naboth, saying, "Give me your vineyard that I may have it for a _____ garden." 1 Kings 21: 2

Best Foot Forward

Bible Reading: Acts 3

Memory Verse: Count yourselves dead to sin but alive to God in Christ Jesus. Therefore do not let sin reign in your mortal body so that you obey its evil desires. Romans 6:11–12

As I was rushing to board a bus in London. My foot caught the kerb and I fell. Not too much damage was done but my foot became more and more painful and I found it difficult to walk.

The foot is a very complex structure – lots of small bones and ligaments all working together to help us to run, jump, stand on tiptoe, kick a ball and lots of other things.

My foot was much better the next morning after a good rest but the experience made me thankful for the ability to walk and run and jump.

Peter and John went to the temple in Jerusalem to pray. A man who was lame from birth was sitting begging. He expected Peter and John to give him some money. Peter

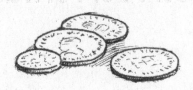

said to him, "Silver and gold I do not have; but what I do have I give you: In the name of Jesus Christ of Nazareth, rise up and walk."

He lifted him up and immediately his feet and ankles received strength. The man went into the temple with Peter and John. He was walking and leaping and praising God. How good it would have felt to use his feet for the first time. He remembered to praise God for that gift. Do we?

When walking is mentioned in the Bible, it often means our whole way of life or behaviour. Our feet carry us into different situations – good or evil. How important to be guided by God's word in all that we do and everywhere we go. "Your word is a lamp to my feet and a light to my path." Psalm 119:105.

The Lord promises needed strength to all who wait upon him. "They shall run and not be weary," he says, "and they shall walk and not faint" Isaiah 40:31.

Nowadays we so often use a car or bike or bus to get anywhere, but in Bible times, when most travelling was done on foot, people would know very well how soon weariness and tiredness would overcome the traveller. In the journey of life our strength is from the Lord God.

Habakkuk says "The Lord God is my strength, he will make my feet like deer's feet, and he will make me walk on my high hills" (3:19).

In eastern lands long ago the traveller's feet would get very dirty and dusty in their open sandals. A sign of hospitality was to wash the visitor's feet when he came to the house. This would usually be done by a servant. After Jesus and his disciples had the Passover meal in the upper room in Jerusalem, Jesus took a basin of water and a towel and washed the disciples' feet. This was a wonderful example to them and to us of love and service to others. We can show that love and service in many different ways – even by giving a cup of cold water, Jesus says.

So let us be thankful for our feet and use them to walk in ways that are pleasing to God.

REMEMBER TO PRAY

ACTS: Adoration. Confession. Thanks. Supplication.

BIBLE SEARCH

Find the missing words in the verses. The initials of your answers will spell out a phrase found in the Third Epistle of John verse 4.

1. If I then, your Lord and Teacher, have washed your feet; you also aught to _____ one another's feet. John 13: 14

2. You shall walk in ____ the ways which the Lord your God has commanded you... Deuteronomy 5: 33

3. The blind see and the _____ walk; the lepers are cleansed, and the deaf hear; the dead are raised up and the poor have the gospel preached to them. Matthew 11: 5

4. For the Lord will be your confidence, and will _____ your foot from being caught. Proverbs 3: 26

5. Vindicate me, O LORD, For I have walked in my _____. I have also trusted in the LORD; I shall not slip. Psalm 26: 1

6. But if one walks in the _____ he stumbles because the light is not in him. John 11: 10

7. How beautiful upon the mountains are the feet of him who brings good news, who proclaims peace, who brings glad _____ of good things, who proclaims salvation, who says to Zion, 'Your God reigns!'. Isaiah 52: 7

8. Those who wait on the Lord shall renew their strength...they shall ____ and not be weary. Isaiah 40: 31

9. I will walk in your truth:_____ my heart to fear your name. Psalm 86: 11

10. Every place on which the sole of your foot _____ shall be yours. Deuteronomy 11: 24

11. In their hands they shall bear you up, lest you _____ your foot against a stone. Psalm 91: 12

Answer ——————   ————   ——————————

Ears to Hear

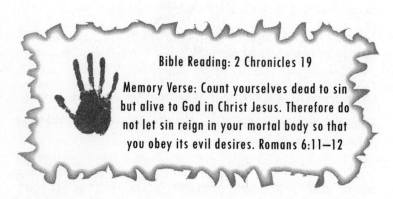

Bible Reading: 2 Chronicles 19

Memory Verse: Count yourselves dead to sin but alive to God in Christ Jesus. Therefore do not let sin reign in your mortal body so that you obey its evil desires. Romans 6:11–12

We are surrounded today by all sorts of noise. In the home we can hear the washing machine, the vacuum cleaner or radio. In the town the constant hum of the car engine or the screech of brakes or hooting horns mean that it is never silent. Even in the quiet countryside we hear the birds singing or a sheep bleating or a river trickling over the stones.

But do we ever stop to think of the wonderful gift of hearing that God has given us? What pleasure we receive in hearing beautiful music or the laughter of a little baby. What a blessing it is to hear the warning sound of a fire alarm or a big lorry reversing. How good it is to hear the loving voice of your mother or father.

It is vitally important that we use the ear that God has given us to hear his word. "He that has ears to hear, let him hear," said Jesus.

The promise of salvation is given to those who call on the name of the Lord (Romans 10:13). But how shall they call on him in whom they have not believed? And how shall they believe in him of whom they have not heard? And how shall they hear without a preacher? (Romans 10:14).

The hearing of God's word preached is a vital part of what God uses to bring sinners to himself. But even those who are dull of hearing or deaf can still 'hear' God's word as he communicates the good news of Jesus Christ to their understanding.

It is important to remember that God also hears. When Hezekiah had a big problem he brought it to the Lord in prayer. "Lord," he said, "bow down thine ear and hear."

Nehemiah prayed, "Let your ear be attentive that you may hear the prayer of your servant." God heard and answered their prayers.

How good to be like young Samuel who heard God's voice speaking to him and replied, "Speak, for your servant hears." May we be hearing what God the Lord speaks to us.

REMEMBER TO PRAY

ACTS: Adoration. Confession. Thanks. Supplication.

BIBLE SEARCH

Find the missing words from the verses.

1. Jesus said, Hear me _____ , and understand. Mark 7: 14

2. You go near and hear ____ that the Lord our God may say. Deuteronomy 5: 27

3. Whoever hears these sayings of mine, and does them, I will liken him to a wise man, who built his house on the _____. Matthew 7: 24

4. And Samuel answered "_____ for your servant hears." 1 Samuel 3: 10

5. Cause me to hear your lovingkindness in the morning; for in you do I _____. Psalm 143: 8

6. If you heed the commandments of the Lord your God, which I command you today and are careful to _____ them. Deuteronomy 28: 13

7. The _____ ear and the seeing eye, the Lord has made them both. Proverbs 20: 12

8. Come near you nations, to hear; and heed, you people! Let the _____ hear and all that is in it. Isaiah 34: 1

9. All the people were very _____ to hear him. Luke 19: 48

10. Draw near to hear _____ than to give the sacrifice of fools, for they do not know that they do evil. Ecclesiastes 5: 1

The initial letters of your answers will spell out the words missing from the following verse.

He who has _____ ___ _____ let him hear. Matthew 11: 15

God Gave Me Eyes

Bible Reading: Mark 10

Memory Verse: Count yourselves dead
to sin but alive to God in Christ Jesus.
Therefore do not let sin reign in your
mortal body so that you obey its evil
desires. Romans 6:11–12

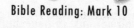

I have to go to the optician regularly to get new glasses because my eyesight is not as good as it used to be. I can no longer read the numbers in the telephone directory without the help of my glasses. How I appreciate my glasses but how much more should I appreciate the gift of eyesight itself.

The eye is an amazingly complex and intricate organ receiving messages and transmitting them to our brain. We are able to see where we are going, to notice any approaching dangers, to admire the beauty of our surroundings, to see the expressions on the faces of our family and friends. All these are wonderful blessings from God our creator – he made our eyes – and gave us the gift of eyesight.

Perhaps we never think about the gift of eyesight – we take it for granted. A friend of mine has just had an operation to remove a fine film from the surface of her eye. This is called a cataract. Her vision had become blurred and she could hardly read. What a difference after her operation. How she appreciates the gift of eyesight.

Blind Bartimaeus sat by the roadside begging. He shouted out to Jesus as he walked along the road. Jesus called him over. "What do you want?" Jesus asked him. "Lord, that I might receive my sight," was his reply. What a difference that must have made to his life.

God who formed the eye, can see everything that we do. Nothing is hidden from him. The eyes of the Lord are in every place, we are told in the book of Proverbs, beholding the evil and the good. This should affect how we live and how we use our eyes. What we see has a big impact on our minds. We should be careful that we read only what is pure and wholesome. We should be selective about what we watch on the television. Jesus describes the eye as the light of the body. If your eye is pure, your whole body will be full of light. But if your eye is evil then your whole body will be full of terrible darkness. We should ask the Lord who made our eyes, to keep our vision pure and pleasing to him, remembering that he sees everything.

Thank God for your eyesight but also ask him for spiritual eyesight. "Open my eyes that I may see wondrous things from your law," is a good prayer to have as we read God's word. This does not refer to our physical eyes but to the understanding of our minds.

Blind Bartimaeus' eyes were opened so that he could see Jesus. It is vital that the "eyes" of our souls are opened so that we can see Jesus in a spiritual way and love him and follow him.

REMEMBER TO PRAY

ACTS: Adoration. Confession. Thanks. Supplication.

BIBLE SEARCH

Find the missing words from the verses. Your answers will spell out the name of the gift that God has given us.

1. Turn away my _____ from looking at worthless things. Psalm 119: 37

2. The eyes of the Lord your God are always on *the land*, from the beginning of the _____ to the very end of the year. Deuteronomy 11: 12

3. The eyes of the Lord which scan to and fro throughout the whole _____ . Zechariah 4: 10

4. One thing I know: that though I was blind, now I ____. John 9: 25

5. Jesus ... touched their eyes. And _____ their eyes received sight and they followed him. Matthew 20: 34

6. The people who walked in darkness have seen a _____ light; those who dwelt in the land of the shadow of death, upon them a light has shined. Isaiah 9: 2

7. O God .... My sins are not _____ from you. Psalm 69: 5

8. Open my eyes, that I may see wondrous _____ from your law. Psalm 119: 18

Answer _____

Hands Up!

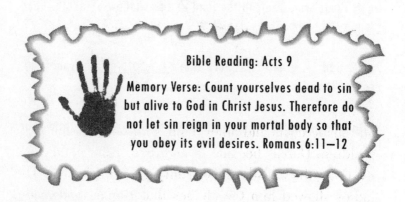

Bible Reading: Acts 9

Memory Verse: Count yourselves dead to sin but alive to God in Christ Jesus. Therefore do not let sin reign in your mortal body so that you obey its evil desires. Romans 6:11–12

We use our hands in so many ways. Can you think of any? We shake hands when we meet someone. When we say goodbye to a friend we will wave our hand in the air. A little child crossing the road will want the security of his father's hand. It is nice just to hold the hand of someone we love.

We clap our hands together when we are happy or when we want to applaud what someone else has done. We use our hands to write, or do crafts or use a tool, to carry, to point. The list goes on and on. The good uses of our hands are many and varied.

We read in the book of Acts about a lady who put her hands to good use. Dorcas was always doing good deeds for her needy neighbours. She was good at sewing

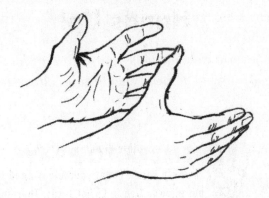

and made coats and other clothes for widows and their children. Dorcas became ill and died. Her friends sent for Peter the apostle. Peter came to Dorcas' room. The ladies showed him the clothes that Dorcas had made. Peter put everyone else out of the room, knelt down and prayed. He spoke to Dorcas and immediately she sat up fit and able to use her hands to help more people.

It is possible to use our hands for bad purposes - to steal what does not belong to us, or to cause pain by slapping or punching.

Achan caused a great deal of trouble to himself, his family and his whole nation by using his hands wickedly. He stole a beautiful garment, some silver and gold from the spoils of the battle of Jericho and hid them under his tent. This was expressly against God's commands. The nation of Israel lost the next battle. Joshua their leader had to deal strictly with the cause of the problem. The thief Achan and his family were destroyed – all because of using his hands wrongly.

Idleness is not commended in God's word either. Those who are idle become poor we are told in Proverbs. "Whatsoever your hand finds to do, do it with your might," is the good advice of the Preacher in Ecclesiastes.

REMEMBER TO PRAY

ACTS: Adoration. Confession. Thanks. Supplication.

BIBLE SEARCH

Find the missing words. The initial letters will spell out how Ecclesiastes 9: 10 tells us to use our hands. It is with your _____.

1. As the eyes of servants look to the hand of their _____ ...so our eyes look to the Lord our God. Psalm 123: 2

2. His hands full of sweet _____ beaten fine. Leviticus 16: 12

3. They set their hands to this _____ work. Nehemiah 2: 18

4. She stretches out her hands to the distaff, and her hand _____ the spindle. Proverbs 31: 19

5. She said to herself, "If only I may _____ his garment, I shall be made well." Matthew 9: 21

Learning to Swim

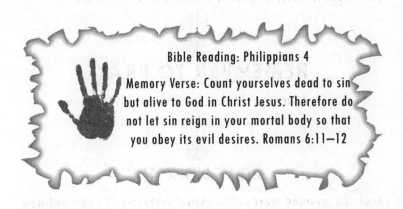

Bible Reading: Philippians 4

Memory Verse: Count yourselves dead to sin but alive to God in Christ Jesus. Therefore do not let sin reign in your mortal body so that you obey its evil desires. Romans 6:11-12

Have you learned how to swim yet? Perhaps when you go to the swimming pool you look at the water and are afraid that you would sink to the bottom and drown? You need to have confidence that the water will hold you up. Relax and launch out with gentle strokes at first. It would be a mistake to struggle and flail about. Once you have that confidence to relax and float or swim you realise that the water will hold you up next time too. The more relaxed you become, the more enjoyable swimming becomes.

I learned to swim long ago in the sea one summer. My father put his hand under my chin to keep my head out of the water and told me what to do with my arms and legs. I knew he would not let me come to any harm and once I got my feet off the ground I realised I was swimming. The first thing I had to learn to do was to rest confidently in my father.

The Christian life is a bit like that too. The saved soul has to rest secure and confident in Christ – confident that he is holding us and will keep us. Faith and repentance are gifts that God gives to his people. With the help of God the Holy Spirit we launch out in faith, trusting in the finished work of Christ.

It is a mistake to struggle and try to work at things ourselves. Progress in the Christian life comes by resting in the Lord, and trusting in him. "I can do all things," said Paul, "through Christ who strengthens me." "Without him I can do nothing."

It can be quite amusing to see the different styles of swimmers in the pool. Some are graceful; some make a lot of splashing. Some are slow; others race through the water. But all are swimming and making progress.

There are many different kinds of people in God's family of believers. Some work quietly, almost unnoticed. Others are more prominent. Progress is made at different rates and in different ways. The important factor is that through faith in Christ, progress is being made.

REMEMBER TO PRAY

ACTS: Adoration. Confession. Thanks. Supplication.

BIBLE SEARCH

Find the missing words from these verses. The initials of your answers will spell out the subject of the story.

1. Looking unto Jesus the author and _____ of our faith. Hebrews 12: 2

2. Let us draw near with a true heart in full _____ of faith. Hebrews 10:22

3. But without faith it is _____ to please him: for he who comes to God must believe that he is, and that he is a rewarder of those who diligently seek him. Hebrews 11:6

4. And _____ I have the gift of prophecy, and understand all mysteries, and all knowledge; and though I have all faith, so that I could remove mountains, but have not love, I am nothing. I Corinthians 13: 2

5. So then faith comes by _____ and hearing by the word of God. Romans 10:17

6. That you do not become sluggish, but imitate those who through faith and patience _____ the promises. Hebrews 6:12

7. And his _____ through faith in his name has made this man strong, whom you see and know. Acts 3:16

8. I found it necessary to write to you exhorting you to _____ earnestly for the faith which was once for all delivered to the saints Jude 1: 3

9. Therefore, as we have opportunity, let us do good to all, especially to those who are of the _____ of faith. Galatians 6:10

10. But to him who does not work, but believes on him who justifies the ungodly, his faith is accounted for _____. Romans 4:5

11. And the apostles said unto the Lord, "_____ our faith." Luke 17:5

12. Now faith is the _____ of things hoped for, the evidence of things not seen. Hebrews 11:1

13. Above all, _____ the shield of faith, with which you will be able to quench all the fiery darts of the wicked one. Ephesians 6:16

Answer _____   _____   _____

Our Sense of Smell

Bible Reading: John 12

Memory Verse: Count yourselves dead to sin
but alive to God in Christ Jesus. Therefore do
not let sin reign in your mortal body so that
you obey its evil desires. Romans 6:11–12

O ne of the five senses that God has given us is the sense of smell - one that perhaps we take for granted - but very useful nevertheless.

Do you ever find that a particular smell can suddenly make you think of something that happened long ago? Perhaps the smell of a certain flower can make you remember a special time or place? Every time I go into a garden with a box hedge, the distinctive smell immediately takes me back to my grandmother's garden where I often played as a little child. The sense of smell brings back happy memories.

Smell can also warn of danger. If gas is leaking from the pipe, the first warning of danger comes through our nose. The smell of burning too warns us that a coal has fallen from the fire or that out dinner is going to spoil.

We get so much pleasure from the beautiful scent of a flower, or some fruit or the ozone at the sea-side.

Without our sense of smell we would not enjoy our food so much. We would not taste it so well and we would not have such a good appetite.

Some smells are not pleasant and make us turn away - milk that has gone sour and is not fit to drink or food that has gone bad. That stops us eating something that might harm us.

When Isaac was an old blind man his son Jacob wanted to get the blessing due to the elder brother Esau. He dressed up in Esau's clothes which had the smell of the fields on them. Isaac was unsure of Jacob's voice but when he smelled Esau's clothes he was sure he was blessing Esau.

When the children of Israel offered burnt sacrifices to God on the altar as Moses had commanded them, the sacrifices are described as being a sweet savour (or smell) to the Lord. This was pleasing to God.

These sacrifices have been abolished. There is no need for them now for Jesus Christ offered himself once and for all as the perfect sacrifice on Calvary. "Walk in love, as Christ also has loved us and has given himself for us as an offering and a sacrifice to God for a sweet smelling savour." This sacrifice was satisfying and pleasing to God like a beautiful perfume.

Our sacrifice of praise is pleasing to God. He wants our prayers to rise up to him like a sweet smelling perfume. In God's revelation to John on Patmos he saw the twenty four elders falling down before the Lamb (Jesus) – each one with a harp and a golden bowl full of odours or perfumes, which are the prayers of the saints.

Mary poured a box of precious perfumed ointment over the feet of Jesus. She was criticized for this extravagant gesture but Jesus was pleased with her expression of love for him. Mary gave Jesus her most treasured possession. Should we not follow her example and give to Jesus our soul, our life, our all.

REMEMBER TO PRAY

ACTS: Adoration. Confession. Thanks. Supplication.

BIBLE SEARCH

Find the missing words. The initial letters will spell out the part of your body that is connected with the sense of smell.

1. They have ears, but they do not hear; _____ they have, but they do not smell. Psalm 115: 6

2. You shall burn the whole ram on the altar. It is a burnt _____ . Exodus 29: 18

3. It is a regular burnt offering, which was ordained at Mount Sinai for a _____ aroma, an offering made by fire to the Lord. Numbers 28: 6

4. The vines with the _____ grapes give a good smell. Song of Solomon 2: 13

5. And so it shall be: Instead of a sweet smell there will be a stench... Instead of a _____ robe, a girding of sackcloth; and branding instead of beauty. Isaiah 3:24-25

6. Let my prayer be set forth before you as _____, The lifting up of my hands as the evening sacrifice. Psalm 141: 2

7. And walk in _____ as Christ also has loved us. Ephesians 5: 2

Answer _____

Play by the Rules

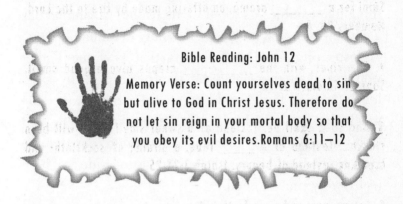

Bible Reading: John 12

Memory Verse: Count yourselves dead to sin but alive to God in Christ Jesus. Therefore do not let sin reign in your mortal body so that you obey its evil desires. Romans 6:11–12

Every game has rules and if you want to enjoy it you have to obey the rules. If you break a rule, the referee stops the game and you might get sent off. A referee isn't there to spoil the game – just try playing football without one. It would be chaos. The referee and the rules are there to make the game fun.

God has given us rules to live by: The Ten Commandments. *Do not worship any other god. Do not make any idols. Do not use God's name in vain. Remember to keep the Sabbath day holy. Honour you father and mother. Do not murder. Do not commit adultery. Do not steal. Do not lie. Do not covet.*

God's rules are there to make life better. Just as a football match is no fun without rules, so life becomes miserable if we do not obey God's rules. God's word tells us what he requires. So never take the Bible for granted. It is a great mercy to hear God's word preached and explained. God's word works on our conscience – that thing that troubles us when we do wrong. No animal has a conscience. God has given this only to human beings.

Jesus promised his followers that God the Father would send another Comforter, the Holy Spirit. He would teach them all things and bring to the remembrance the words that Jesus had said. It is important for us to read God's word and to try to memorise it and to pray that the Holy Spirit would bring it to our minds to guide and help us in every time of need.

REMEMBER TO PRAY

ACTS: Adoration. Confession. Thanks. Supplication.

BIBLE SEARCH

Find the missing words. The initial letters of the answers spell out some good advice for us.

1. All that the Lord has said we will do and be _____.
Exodus 24: 7

2. So they read distinctly from the _____, in the law of God.
Nehemiah 8: 8

3. Give ____ to the law of our God... Isaiah 1: 10

4. Stand fast therefore in the liberty by which Christ has made us free and do not be entangled again with a _____ of bondage. Galatians 5: 1

5. I will instruct you and _____ you in the way you should go. Psalm 32: 8

6. But be doers of the word and not _____ only. James 1: 22

7. The commandment of the Lord is pure, _____ the eyes. Psalm 19:8

8. Till I come give attention to _____ , to exhortation to doctrine. 1 Timothy 4:13

9. Do not my words do good to him who walks _____ . Micah 2:7

10. A new commandment I give unto you, That you _____ one another. John 13:34

11. Open my _____, that I may see wondrous things from your law. Psalm 119:18

12. If anyone _____ me, let him follow me; and where I am, there my servant will be also. John 12:26

Answer _____   _____   _____

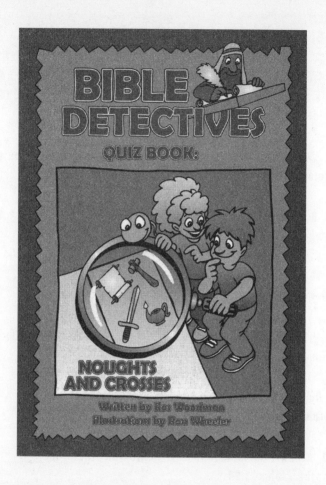

Come join the Bible Detectives, Harry, Jess and Click the mouse as they negotiate the stories and pages of the Bible.

These quizzes are designed for group use in kids clubs, Sunday schools and families. With material that is appropriate for a variety of ages this is a book that you will all enjoy.

ISBN: 978-1-84550-081-8

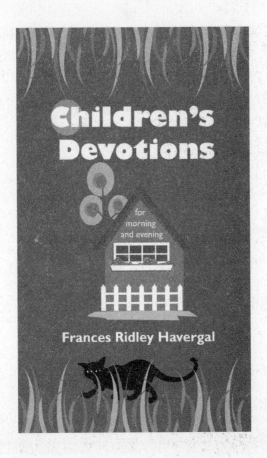

Frances Ridley Havergal is a famous hymn writer who also wrote gospel stories for children. Here are a months worth of devotions for morning and evening. Each devotional story has a scripture and a short poem to think about. They are perfect for family devotion times be it in the morning or last thing at night.

ISBN: 978-1-85792-973-7

CHRISTIAN FOCUS PUBLICATIONS

Christian Focus   **Christian Heritage**   **CF4K**   **Mentor**

Christian Focus Publications publishes books for adults and children under its four main imprints: Christian Focus, CF4K, Mentor and Christian Heritage. Our books reflect that God's word is reliable and Jesus is the way to know him, and live for ever with him.

Our children's publication list includes a Sunday School curriculum that covers pre-school to early teens; puzzle and activity books. We also publish personal and family devotional titles, biographies and inspirational stories that children will love.

If you are looking for quality Bible teaching for children then we have an excellent range of Bible story and age specific theological books.

From pre-school to teenage fiction, we have it covered!

Find us at our web page:
www.christianfocus.com

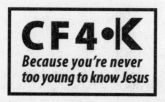

CF4•K
Because you're never too young to know Jesus